Sex Good or Bad?

End the cycle of toxic encounters and create a loving and fulfilling relationship

F G Fraser

First edition published by WOW Book Publishing™ and

Vishal Morjaria at WowBookPublishing.com

www.MasterYourWow.com

Copyright © Francesca Fraser

ISBN: 9798386217198

Warning—Disclaimer

Table of Contents

Sex: Good or Bad?

Dedication

I experienced many toxic encounters and failed relationships throughout my young life which all ended in me feeling pained, tormented, confused, and even victimised. Eventually, the pain got too much, and I finally discovered the knowledge and tools that helped me in all areas of my life and even got me married to a wonderful man. I am keen to share the knowledge and tools with you, so as to prevent you from continuing to go round in your own vicious circles. I also tell you many of my own real-life stories before realising what mistakes I made and I explain what I would have done differently, knowing what I know now, in case you ever find your own self in that same situation.

Writing this book has also been an important part of my healing journey.

A happy self = a happy relationship.

A happy relationship = happy children.

Happy children = A happy and peaceful world.

About the Author

Francesca was born in Brighton on 14th August 1986 making her 36 in 2022.

After a lot of stressful and traumatic moments; some of which you will get to read about in this book; Francesca is now successfully married to a wonderful man that treats her amazingly. He has given her the ultimate commitment she had craved for, for an incredibly long time.

She enjoys boxing, swimming, taking long walks in nature and she loves doing yoga too. Francesca loves securing acting roles here and there, as well as being put in the background of films and music videos. She has worked along-side some huge names in the film and music industry.

She let one Hollywood star hold her hand; she smiled and had eye contact with another; another one stood awfully close next to her, he couldn't have stood closer or more perpendicular without touching her!

On set with a huge music artist, he came over to her and started a conversation with her about the paintings on the wall, a conversation that she had already just been discussing with the guy next to her. Had he been watching her?!?!

Francesca has incredibly attractive energy, and she can't wait to take you on a rollercoaster of a ride with her book as well as give you helpful tips and advice to help you in your own life!

To my Wonderful reader.
Please read.

Thank you for picking up my book and taking the time to read it. You will not be bored!

I wanted to let you know that there may be some parts of this book that may make you feel uncomfortable. Please don't shy away from these uncomfortable feelings but allow them to be there. Watch them and watch your thoughts and feelings as closely as you can.

You are not your thoughts, and you are not your feelings. Take a slow and deep breath. How did your thoughts and feelings respond to that sentence?

"You are not your thoughts, and you are not feelings."

The idea of being super aware and conscious of your thoughts and feelings is so that they can dissolve and disappear and not create any dramas or conflicts in yourself that may go on and cause drama and conflict elsewhere in the world, specifically in your close relationships.

Everything I have written is from my own perspective and what I have learnt on my own excruciating and confusing journey and what has helped me. I cannot guarantee everything will be spot on in all circumstances, so anything you do try in this book is solely down to you to take responsibility for.

Thank you so much for your amazing presence in the world. I LOVE YOU!

The Boring Bit...

Thank You

Thank YOU for living your life, because without you choosing to read this book there would be no point in writing it.

Thank you, Alfie Fraser-wenham for being the most perfect baby, the sweetest cheeky little boy that is growing into such a lovely young man and for being a lifesaving son.

I would like to thank my wonderful, amazing husband Adnan for supporting me and loving me through the process of writing this book. Without him and the comfort and safety of his love and loving family, this book would not have been possible.

Thank you, Christine Flynn, mine, and Alfie's Nan, for always being there for us both throughout the years; for showing us love and care and for all the games and chats we have had and being good company.

Thank you, Mum, for choosing to be with kind caring men; for giving birth to me and raising me the best way you knew how to. I was not the easiest of daughters.

Thank you, Emily and Clemi Fraser for being my lovely sisters and for giving me lovely memories in childhood.

Thank you, Sonia Ashworth, my Godmother for being one of the loveliest people I have ever known and being in my life since the moment I took my first breath in this fascinating world. Thank you for filming mum's caesarean so I could watch myself being born, a bit weird but cool.

Thank you to the Mabry family, Sallie, Keith and Paige for always helping me when whenever I asked and fostering me for two weeks when I was eighteen. I will love you forever!

Thank you, Katie Broad for being one of my greatest ever friends and giving me longest real true connection with another beautiful being in this crazy world. I love you more than you could possibly know.

Thank you, Deborah Jay Kelly, for seeing the good in me and showing me lots of care on my journey and trusting me to be a model in your book series, "Model Diaries." You have helped increase my confidence tremendously, and I have met so many wonderful people along the way. I love you dearly and I am so grateful and relieved to have you in my life.

Thank you, Ben Chai, for being interested in my book, helping me edit some of chapters, and for the lovely warm and safe hugs at Deborah's birthday parties. LOVELY HUG!

Thank you, Sue Johnson for the two soothing reiki healing sessions we had, both leading to incredible spiritual experiences!

Thank you, Ben Harman, Jeff Harrison, and Thierry Porter for being dear friends to me on different parts of my life journey, being a comfort, and showing me not all men are scary. I know there are many others but these I feel have been closest to me.

Thank you, Lukas Di Sparrow, for being a fun friend to hang around with when we did, and thank you for teaching me how to use "You Cut" video editor.

Thank you, Stuart Waite, you know everything I am thankful for, you also come under the Gentleman chapter.

Thank you Gatis Kandis, a hilarious comedian that made the semi-finalist on Britain's got Talent, for making me laugh and for all our games of "words with friends". You're good fun to play with!

Thank you, Joshua Neil, we have had many interesting conversations included in the topic of this book. You helped me with a deep-rooted fear of mine and opened my mind to other perspectives. You come under the gentleman chapter of this book.

Thank you, Perry Power for breaking your silence and being a support for survivors everywhere! Big love!

Thank you, Jamie Johnson for introducing me to boxing. You're amazing, and so many people agree! Never forget that!

Thank you, Dorothy Koomson, for all your amazing work! Thank you for your amazing creation "The ice-cream girls" fiction book and all you other incredible books too.

Thank you Alan Davies for writing your own book "Just Ignore him". Inspired me with the one word chapter titles.

Thank you, Anna Bey for your work in teaching women not to give themselves away too freely to men.

Thank you, Adam Mussa, for your soothing work with trauma survivors.

Thank you to Vishal, Pauline, and Alba for being a fabulous supportive team on my book-writing journey. WOW! It is here!

Thank you, Ben Allsop at Shape Your Destiny, for showing me true love, kindness, and patience and that there are good men in the world and for all your wonderful coaching calls and encouragement in writing this book. I haven't always been the easiest person to coach, but you have never given up on me.

Thank you, Simon Lowe, for your presence in the world and for getting your own book out, it no doubt helped encourage me on my own book writing journey.

Thank you, Scott Hilliar for being a gentleman I feel I can connect with.

Thank you, thank you, thank you to the wonderful Philip Chan for being one of the sweetest hearts of my life. Loving me and showing me genuine care and telling me you want to read my book and starting me on my book writing journey. Probably guiding me in spirit too. I know you're resting peacefully; such a kind and wise man with time for everyone no matter what the hour of the day it was.

Thank you to my amazing Dad for being an amazing father

and teaching me so much about the Power some call God and showing me that good men do exist and being a key role model in writing your own book. (I know my dad, the greatest man ever, that taught me true love, and is also resting peacefully, watching over me and guiding me.)

Thank you to my wonderful Stepdad Mike for being another amazing role model and showing me good men exist. Also resting peacefully.

Thank you, Derek Heggie for all your work on mental health and positivity. You do a great job!

Thank you, Brandon Mcconnell, for being what I believed to be a safe space to me for many years.

Thank you, Eckhart Tolle, for your amazing presence in the world and getting me feeling joy, knowing that I am not the only one that knows what you teach. I am not alone in the world. Thank you for keeping me feeling positive on my journey that most definitely, one day I too will write a book.

Thank you, Tony Robbins for all your amazing work helping people overcome tremendous hurdles in their life. I enjoyed the on-line UPW and am excited to attend in real life in July 2023. Thank you, thank you, Thank you!

Thank you, Oprah Winfrey for sharing your personal stories with the world and helping others that struggle and suffer in life.

Rori Raye, thank you, thank you, thank you so much for all your coaching tools, you helped me change my life and you have helped me help others too!

Thank you to all the other relationship coaches that have helped me on my journey, Renee Wade, Helena Hart and Mathew Coast and Steve Harvey.

Another life saver I discovered on YouTube. While I was going through the Twin Flame Hell, is Kurt Johnson, the greatest Twin flame specialist, without you I would not have had the glimmer of light in one of the darkest times of my entire life. Thank You Thank You Thank You!

Thank you, Ed Sheeran, for being a lovely genuine gentleman.

Last and the incredibly amazing most; Thank you so much for the highest almighty power, for saving me every time I call out and for always answering my prayers; and for all the amazing and wonderful souls disguised as people placed on my journey called life that you gifted me. Thank you! I know there are many more incredible encounters to come.

THANK YOU! THANK YOU! THANK YOU!

Testimonials

"Frankie was a rock to me when I was struggling in an abusive relationship. She had a lot of amazing advice and she never got tired of wanting to help me. My abusive ex-husband also called her "fair" while I spoke to her on the phone during an argument. Read her book!"

– Sian Mcsween. Glamour Model. UK.

"Frankie is my wife, and I had no intentions of ever getting married. I was emotionally unavailable, but I love having her in my life. She is a ray of light."

– Adnan, Cyber security, and hotel business owner.

"Frankie is a very charismatic person and wise too. She knows what she is talking about and has a huge heart wanting to help people in distress. She helped me out of a very dark place. Read her book and you will one hundred percent discover something that will help you."

– Omoyemi Fatusin. IT professional, Milton Keynes.

"Francesca is a wise and effective communicator. At a point of my darkness, she helped me embrace the feeling and be comfortable enough to do nothing but wait... wait and listen. This virtual request saved me from an impulsive decision, and I will forever be grateful for her wisdom and love."

– Keneilwe. Digital project manager, Cape Town.

"Frankie is a beautiful soul. She is always willing to help me with anything when I ask and has even done some fashion and beauty modelling for my book series "Model Diaries"!"

– Deborah Jay Kelly, Celebrity Red carpet host, the owner and CEO of The Angel Academy of teaching and Training, Model, and Author.

"Frankie has a lot of compassion for all beings. When I was struggling, she was there for me and helped guide me. For that I will always be grateful!"

– Stuart Waite, Service Advisor from Sittingbourne.

Note to my in-laws

To my incredibly amazing in-laws, firstly I want to thank all of you for welcoming me into your beautiful family. I have been seriously blessed with my new family members. Mashallah!

I would also like to apologise for any of the parts of this book that maybe offensive to you. Adnan was worried about you reading this and wanted me to change it but…

1) I need to do this to own my story, it's part of my healing journey.

2) The truth is immensely powerful in helping people heal and for the world in general. God is the truth, and I mustn't shy away from it however terrifying it may be to be so honest, open and vulnerable.

I recommend you read the first chapter "Heavenly experience". That is one of my favourite chapters.

Foreword

Francesca is a sweet, kind and caring individual, and clearly loves people and helps them in any way possible. She is funny and entertaining, but from what I can tell she hasn't had the best experiences in her past regarding relationships and sex. However, I know she is now successfully married, and she wants to share her knowledge of how she got there.

Francesca has learnt a lot about psychology and by going deep within herself she has found many answers to create a long lasting and loving relationship which she is excited to share with you in this book. Understanding men and their needs as well as her own needs and feelings; both men and women will gain a better understanding of themselves and their love interests or partners from reading this book.

Richard Standeven, Award-winning film director. Many of his impressive Film and TV credits include "Band of Gold." "Falling for a Dancer." "Cracker." "Between the Lines." "Ballykiss Angel" and most recently "Waking the Dead."

Richard has always been a good friend to me, and he has never harmed me and is not the film director I have mentioned in this book!

CHAPTER 1

A Heavenly Experience

In June 2012, the first time I was on set, an award-winning film director took an interest in me. I thought he was just another extra like me, but his friend was the director and had asked him to help on set, so he did. I didn't know he was a film director until he emailed me a few days later and said he was interested in other people's scripts and stories. I got excited and started writing my film script.

While I was writing the film script based on my true-life events, I realised I had a lot of pain and shame in me. I went to the deepest part of me, which connects to whom some call God and others Allah, some may have different names. I vowed to not drink alcohol ever again, eat pork or have sex unless it was with a man I was married to.

I felt the shame and the pain and vowed to never have a sinful thought again and in everything I did I would hold onto God. It was a lonely path to be on. I didn't see many people, only my son.

I decided I was a Muslim, and I was finally purified. I didn't know about praying five times a day or much else. I knew about Ramadan and not drinking alcohol and the basics of being a good human. I decided I needed something to mark it. I had always wondered what it would be like to get a tattoo, but I didn't want anyone to be able to see it. I didn't think a tattoo would suit me and the look I wanted to attain.

I wanted to make my body different. Unseen to any man from

Sex: Good or Bad?

the past and try to purify myself. Injecting ink isn't exactly purifying, but it felt good to me at the time. I got a tattoo under my knicker line; so even in a bikini, no one would be able to see it. It was a symbol between me and God, no man was to come too close to me unless I was married to him.

I even wore a scarf around my head for a couple of days. It felt good to be hidden from sight. I felt safe knowing that no man could see me, and no man would cat call me in the street. I also felt embarrassed because I didn't know anyone else that wore a headscarf. I was on my own. That is why I only lasted a couple of days being fully covered.

I decided that getting a tattoo would be a good ending to my film script, and I added it to the few pages of the outline that I sent to the film director.

I felt so good after I had my tattoo. I felt so calm and clean again. I felt my soul, it was pure. I focussed fully on only having pure, clean thoughts and any unclean thoughts that entered I called out to God to take them away. I did this for a while until I found myself wanting a partner again, a connection, after only a couple of months.

I joined the 'Plenty of Fish' dating site and went on a few dates. I refused to let any man get too close to me though. Even if they were lovely and fanciable. One of the guys I spoke to on Plenty of Fish was incredibly attractive. I felt weak and I didn't trust myself. I also felt a lot of shame when reading the part of his profile that said he didn't like promiscuous women. I believed I had no chance with him at all, and I felt very timid even messaging him!

We were chatting and sending each other messages, then he suggested we become Facebook friends. He told me about his Mum being a Reiki healer and having a group on Facebook. I joined and got chatting with his Mum who had a free meetup group planned. Because I fancied her son it was a huge motivator to get me to travel to his flat in London to see his Mum and have the reiki session. I was more interested in having the reiki session but the excitement that I might see her son made it much more interesting.

I was terrible at planning my train route and I ended up going a super long way around. As a result, I arrived when the group had finished.

There was only one other lady that had attended the group and she had a one-to-one with the handsome man's mother before I arrived.

It was raining hard, and I turned up soaking wet. Even though I was drenched with water I was still super excited to meet this mystical woman that could heal me in some way. When she opened the door, I shone my beaming smile at her.

She introduced herself as Sue and said because there were only two of us and I had turned up late, it was meant to be, and it was important that we both have a one-to-one session.

After Sue put my wet socks on the radiator to dry out and made me a cup of tea we had a chat. I told her about the film director. Sue immediately had bad vibes and told me to stay away from him. Then we started to get into it. She asked me to pick a card from a pack facing downwards.

I chose the Magic card. "Ooo, the Magic card!" She said with mystery.

Sue told me I would experience some Magic within the next couple of days. I had already experienced what I would call magical, so I just brushed it off and thought that it would be like that. I still felt positive because it was always a fantastic experience. When we meditated, I was told to have my feet on the ground and to close my eyes.

As I listened, I heard Sue say the following:

"Imagine a soft warm golden light being poured through the top of your head... It is so beautiful. Imagine it coming down and through your head and past your ears... (then she paused) It gets even more beautiful as it comes down..."

Sex: Good or Bad?

Then there was a longer pause. I imagined this beautiful light coming down and into my stomach, I imagined it coming down.

Suddenly, she spoke again, "Now imagine the light coming down your throat. It gets even more beautiful as it comes down." When she spoke, I felt interrupted and took the light back up to my throat so I could follow her words properly again. I even opened an eye to look at her. This interruption caused me to come out of the meditation. I tried to get back into the meditation and followed her words as best as I could until the end of the meditation.

"Now imagine the light coming down your chest and it is so beautiful. It is coming further down now. Into your stomach Wow! The light is spectacular! There are so many sparkles and whooshing beauty. Wow! It is stunning!"

I did my best to follow her, but the previous interruption had ruined it for me. I can't remember what happened next, but I stayed a little longer with Sue until she had finished her work with me.

The magic that I experienced a couple of nights later was nothing like what I had expected. I had no idea an experience like that could be had while on planet earth. I was asleep in my bed, but it wasn't a dream. It was real. No words will ever be able to describe the experience. Words are from the mind, taken from the physical 3D reality world we all live in. This was something the mind will never be able to comprehend. But even these words cannot explain it, because still, the mind is trying to conceive them into something it can understand.

I will try to explain this experience as closely as I can.

Completely out of nowhere, my usual sleep reality changed.

I didn't know I was asleep when a tiny spec of light caught hold of my awareness and attention. I looked at it curiously, it was new, something to be discovered. I can't really say that I was looking at it because I had no choice to. It was just there. My 3D eye lids weren't open to look at it. It was from the inside.

I stayed asleep, and very gently, smoothly, softly, elegantly, the distant light began to trickle closer towards my individual awareness.

I suppose I could say this light was growing bigger and expanding. I suppose I could see it differently that my individual awareness was going towards it. Wow! I have never seen it like that before. Always the other way because the other way is closer to Sue's words. That is what my mind knows and tries to explain.

It is frustrating trying to use words to describe it, because it is a memory from over a decade ago, November 2012. What I experienced was there in the present moment.

I must continue anyway; the light got bigger, or it trickled into my awareness through the top of my head, more and more, the further it came into me, the more of it I experienced. I saw that it was beautiful, and it made me feel incredibly wonderful.

My mind hadn't butted in, the light was just there, and I started to feel in awe, but unless you experience it, you won't understand the word "awe".

It was so beautiful; it was warm, and it was golden. But those words cannot really explain it, those are still words from the mind and all words taint it. It can never be tainted. That is why there are no words to truly describe it. You wouldn't want to describe it either. You just want to experience it.

The light trickled in further, and it grew more and more intense, but it wasn't intense. It was the opposite of intense, but it was intensely the opposite. It was so overbearingly powerful, but it was so soft and gentle. I had never experienced such heaven on earth before.

My 3D voice inside butted in, "Oh Wow! What is that?" I guess, if my awareness expanded up into the light, my voice may have come from below. Come from my body, which I was still connected to. When it spoke, then my mind was disturbed. Instead of staying still and appreciating every single blissful moment, it remembered my meeting with Sue, the magic card I pulled out and the meditation we did.

Sex: Good or Bad?

It remembered how, when the light came down further into my stomach, how much more amazing and beautiful it became. My mind wanted this light, it wanted this heavenly beauty to smother all corners of its' physical existence, but of course the light could never be physical. It was so beautiful. I tried to grab hold of it as I believed I was my mind. I was greedy for this light, and I wanted all of it straight away.

Unfortunately, the very moment I tried to grasp it, when my mind tried to take control of it, it disappeared quickly. In a flash, faster than the speed of lightening, it was gone. I was in an empty and lonely darkness.

I then woke up in my bed. I was in darkness. All I knew from this experience is that, it was God, heaven, Nirvana. I was in awe, admiration, and wonder.

I sat up in my bed. I stayed still and was afraid to move, afraid to lose the moment. I was in shock too. The gentle kind of shock. That was all I had ever truly wanted and craved intently. Tears gently fell from my eyes and peacefully rolled down my cheeks.

When I was 12, I had a beautiful holiday in the Maldives. I always called that heaven on earth. After experiencing a tiny glimpse of the true meaning of heaven, the Maldives holiday was nothing in comparison.

I believe that my decision to be pure and disconnected from all men and what religion describes as "sin," enabled me to experience a glimpse of heavens' purity.

CHAPTER 2

What do you Truly Desire?

Everyone wants love and connection. Everyone needs love and connection. Where does it come from?

The first experience of love and connection we encounter is as babies from our parents. No one is the perfect parent, but all parents do the best they can with the knowledge and experiences they have. No one is taught to be a parent but there are lots of knowledgeable books and advice-givers out there so parents can do their best. Most parents learn to parent from how they themselves were parented. Either they will copy their parents parenting style or they will do the opposite of their parents parenting style.

How does this affect our adult relationships?

We expect certain things from our significant other and if we don't get it, we can feel unloved and resentful. We are no longer babies; we need to learn to know real love. We are not even taught real love as babies. Love is conditional, we were disciplined and sometimes even punished if we did things our parents did not like. Some children are incredibly lucky, and they do have parents that can make them feel extremely loved. This too can be unsuccessful if they are never taught to do things to help them grow and build healthy life habits when they're older.

It is not an easy ride in the world when it comes to love. Not for anyone. Real true pure love comes from the depth of each and every one of our beings. It is not conditional. "I will love you if you do this, this or this." It just is. However, when we love another, we naturally want to do things that please them. Some people even ignore their own needs to put the other first, this is also not true love as we need to attend to our own selves before loving another.

Some religions say that God is love. Most religions say that God loves all of us and will quickly forgive our sins if we repent.

Human relationships are not always so forgiving when upset occurs from behaviour of the significant other.

Love is beautiful and can feel like ecstasy. Everything seems to go right when we feel in love. When we feel in love, normal everyday mistakes we make don't seem so awful.

We can say I love that item of clothing, car, jewellery, or I love this food. It is not the material object that is the love, but the feeling inside of us that is ignited. We attach it to the clothing, car, or food, if we do that the feeling of love can't last; we eventually want more clothes, an upgrade to a better car or more food.

It is the same when we love a man or a woman. We attach the feeling to them and then that can go stale too when the honeymoon phase wears off and the brain chemicals settle down. We expect them to make us feel a certain way but when they don't, we blame them. That is not real love. We can have a little glimpse of it, but we need to be aware that they don't create that feeling inside, it is already there.

I believe a lot of people have food addictions because it is the first feeling of love we experience as babies. We're all alive because someone cared enough to feed us.

What do you really want?

If you can be honest with yourself deep down, I can guarantee all you really want is a loving long term committed relationship. You want the fairy-tale that Disney films showed us, and other movies showed us when growing up. You, want to feel so in love, get married and live happily ever after.

What do you Truly Desire?

If you take a closer look at why you want that, the reason is to feel safe, loved, cared for, adored, cherished, stable, connected, and certain that you will always have someone to rely on for whatever need you want fulfilled. Also, you believe that if you can get that, then you will be worthy, you will feel worthy and good enough about yourself to finally be happy with yourself.

I am guessing you're reading this book because you haven't found your Mr or Mrs Right, or your Prince that is to be your King or your Princess that will become Queen, and you really would like to. (Or perhaps your're just here to see what naughty stories you find – cheeky!)

(Quick tip – First you must already feel like you are the King or Queen first, to attract it. Or if you don't, which many of us aren't, you can choose to become the King and Queen together with your chosen partner. You can grow together in love. You must never blame your partner for holding you back. You must continue to grow, and if your partner is not willing to grow with you, naturally they will eventually choose to separate, without you ever coming from a place that is not love. I will explain more later in the book.)

Women may dress up sexy, cook their man lovely meals and even have sex with him before getting anything that she really wants from him first.

Men on the other hand you just can't find a woman that isn't dramatic. You need sex, and you can get sex, but you just seem to bump into the woman that is just so dramatic all the time for no reason, you can't understand why? Either that or she seems too weak, too easy to please you and not interesting enough; boring, no spice.

What is stopping you from getting what you want?

You are unable to clearly visualise what you really want, and clouding your vision are lies you have been told, beliefs you have picked up, and negative past experiences, for example:

Sex: Good or Bad?

As a woman, you may believe that ...

- men only want sex

- men only want to commit to a virgin

- you are unlovable

- you have experienced too much trauma

- no man wants you

- men can't handle a strong woman

- you have done terrible things in your past. How can a man love you?

- men are untrustworthy

- where are all the real men?

- he is not "man enough"

- Whereas a man, you may believe that...

    * all Women are just dramatic

    * all Women are gold diggers

    * all Women are too easy and act "slutty"

    * all Women are only good for one thing

There are probably many more items I could list in each category, and the main reason you believe this and have it going on inside you is negative past experiences you have had with many different men or many different women, past cycles repeating themselves.

When we experience negative experiences, it forms a belief and then that belief goes on to repeat itself to then show itself as real. So, how do you get rid of all those negative beliefs? How are you supposed to go out into the world and find a decent partner to love and cherish you and for you to love and cherish them back?

What do you Truly Desire?

Because of your negative beliefs, I can guess that when you are around a man or woman, you find it hard to relax.

Women:

You're afraid the man you like will see your vulnerabilities and he will hurt you... again! The truth is being closed and not showing your true feelings, pretending to be "cool" is what is hurting you when it comes to being with a man.

Too many of us have been taught that we need to be cool and not show our true feelings, we must never be dramatic!

When you don't express your feelings, that is what creates you to be overly dramatic later and do things you wouldn't do when feeling the in love feeling. Feeling your true feelings can be scary, especially in front of a man you have feelings for and don't want to lose. I will teach you how to be open to your true feelings in a later chapter, "Feelings."

Men:

I am guessing you find it hard to relax because something feels a bit off. Something isn't quite right. Is she going to start being dramatic? Or perhaps you just like to feel you're in control because you believe women are only good for one thing? Or perhaps you find it easy to pull women and wonder how easy is this one going to be? Or perhaps you really like her and can't believe you're actually on a date with her?

Sex: Good or Bad?

CHAPTER 3

Feelings

The reason you get into a relationship is because you want to feel good. Sex is intimate and is the closest you can ever be with someone, and it can feel very good.

To get the desired person you want to have sex with, you need to know how to make them feel good and get them into the mood.

It is all to do with feelings and feeling good. For anyone to feel good the underlying feeling someone needs to feel is safe. Creating safety is extremely important. The first thing you need to feel, is safety in yourself and good feelings in yourself. You need to have a genuine sense of feeling that you will be fine without a man or woman in your life. This is ultra-important if you are attempting to pull a member of the opposite sex. If you get rejected, you already know you will be fine without them.

An open warm friendly smile goes a long way in any interaction, with any human being but it is exceptionally important with a love interest you may have. If the smile is genuine and you're already feeling good (warm in the heart) and you're not doing it as a pretence to gain something, then it should always be received well. If it isn't then the person, you're smiling at may have bad experiences in the past or their ego is telling them it is wrong to interact because they're already taken or some other issue. You must remember it has nothing to with you, and you must continue to feel your heart open, warm and loving, just not with that specific individual.

Sex: Good or Bad?

To be attractive to the opposite sex, you need to feel good and be able to create that for yourself within. You need to have hobbies and goals that you're pursuing. I know many people reading this may be suffering from mental health but even so, there are ways you can better yourself and feel better about yourself. You can't be moping around wondering why no one wants to be with you. There will be someone out there that will fit you perfectly even if you do have a mental health condition like depression.

What can you do to feel good?

- Take yourself out for coffee or some other beverage

- Go to the cinema (yes even if you're alone)

- Meet up with friends.

- Take up a new exercise class (I recently discovered I love boxing!)

- Find an online course you're interested in

- Read books.

- Go for walks in nature.

- Have a spa evening at home or if you're lucky, in a salon.

- Get your nails done – Women (or men can have a pedi-cure, why not? I recently read a book about an extremely well-paid coach that gets his toenails painted black with white exclamation marks.)

- Bake a cake or some other cooking, for yourself or family members, (women -not a man unless you get the ring on your finger! Or at least not unless you're doing it from a place of knowing it won't get a long-term commitment!) (Men - wow the lady you have your eye on but don't expect anything in return. Remember we're creating safety.)

When you take yourself out dress up to feel good for yourself as if you were going on a date. You are on a date, with you! You're, dressing up for you and not the significant other.

When you're home alone you can dress up sexily for yourself. Feel good in your body, but don't be attempted to post photos on social media to attract the opposite sex. This is never a smart idea for men or women. It will attract the wrong kind of connection you're after, which I will talk about in another chapter. You can always dress well, feel good and be covered up. In fact, you will feel better and more comfortable if you're covered up. The reason many people dress with skin on show is because they feel insecure. They know they have a good body, so they want to show it to feel more confident. I used to do it.

If you do expose a lot of skin and you come across someone that is naturally confident and they look at you and aren't afraid of reacting, you will automatically feel exposed, and your insecurities will start to show.

I was walking through town one day, and I saw a man with tiny gym shorts on and huge muscley thighs, "wow!" I thought. I could see him squirm and feel uncomfortable when he knew I was "wowing" at him. And some people may not "wow" in a good way.

If you're the kind of person that isn't insecure when someone stares at you, you may feel annoyed that they are "ogling" at you. However, if you do look good, know it, and feel it, it is human nature for others to stare at you, even if you are covered up.

It is not fair on some others either, because many will have an instant attraction and want to get closer to you. It will draw out their unpleasant feeling of not feeling good in themselves, not good enough and therefore, unable to approach you and make that connection that you desire. You miss out too. Some brave individuals may even get an ego rejection which will feel unpleasant, and some may even say unkind things in an attack.

If you feel your body is all you are worth, then you have deep inner healing to do and should cover up and find yourself that isn't your body or the way you look. In the summer months, I do like to have a bit of skin on show, but that is merely because it is a hot day.

When I am feeling safe and with my husband, at times I may like to dress a little sexier, but I feel safe knowing that people can see that I am a taken woman.

If you often like to dress to impress and you wouldn't be seen anywhere without looking good, try doing the opposite and then go out somewhere. It will help you feel into the vulnerable place inside you, where all of your deepest feelings come from.

However, if you're the kind of person that always dresses down and doesn't make much of an effort, try it. Put make-up on and a new dress or another outfit, style your hair. When you go out, you too will get to the vulnerable feeling place.

The idea is to get out of your comfort zone of how you usually dress, so you feel uncomfortably vulnerable and exposed. Don't resist this feeling but embrace it. Notice it. let it be.

Let's go a little deeper

I saw a beautiful heart-touching Facebook post the other day aimed at men. It was saying how men are mostly shut off from their feelings and they rely on women to do the feeling. They lie to themselves and believe that women are better at feeling so leave it up to the woman.

It was saying that the men that continue to not get in touch and feel comfortable with their emotions will stay alone and resent emotions, women and "the feminine" when, it's all an externalized rejected part of themselves. It continued to explain that isn't their fault they can't feel anything, but it is their responsibility to learn how to feel. The post was written by Jayson Gaddis.

Even though many men are afraid of a deeply feeling woman, they don't want to know about feelings or acknowledge them and some will even gas light another which is an abuse tactic people with narcissistic personality disorder use.

The reason some men are afraid of feelings is because

they're logical, they like to fix and solve problems. This doesn't require feelings. A man that loves a woman and is committed to her wants to solve all her problems, so when she isn't feeling good and he can't solve it or it requires hard work on his part, then he will shy away and close himself off. Call her "dramatic." She may have become dramatic because he wasn't able to listen to her feelings in the first place or she came across a man in the past that made her not safe to feel her feelings.

When a woman can truly and authentically feel her feelings, it makes a man feel safe. He feels safe because she is being authentic. The post felt good to me, and I assume to many other women, that it says men need to learn to feel their feelings; however, as women are seen to be the feminine feelers, it is important for women to feel too.

If a woman doesn't feel safe with a man, she will be closed off from her feelings. Trauma response, freeze mode. So, if a man reading this is attracted to a woman he is with, he needs to make her feel safe, as mentioned earlier in this chapter. Feeling good, means feeling safe. If a woman feels safe to feel her feelings, then a man will feel safe, and he can then start to practice feeling his feelings. If a woman does feel afraid it can have a magical effect if she is able to communicate it and feel it effectively.

I remember a time I got onto a busy tube train and a man I sat on the empty seat next to, had tattoos including on his neck. He had the vibe that I had come across too many times that told me he was abusive. He was being friendly and smiling at me in a creepy manner and trying to chat me up. He was being very forward. I was polite and friendly back to him in fear of being rude. There were other passengers around, so I knew I wasn't in total danger.

I surrendered and I told him from the deepest place, vulnerable and authentic, "I feel afraid." He lent back and pulled himself away from me. His next sentence was, "what game are you playing?" I giggled, blushing, feeling nervous that he had seen me. I was only being honest and authentic. I then realised he had been chatting to the girl next to me. When she got off the train, he fol-

Sex: Good or Bad?

lowed her. As he was about to get off the train he said to me, "stay blessed."

In the past when I had encountered men like that, I always ended up getting too close and getting burned, just because I wanted to be polite. I was also incredibly young, and that dangerous vibe made me feel excited. I am pleased I am far away from ever feeling like that ever again though. I did learn hard way.

When you find someone, you are attracted to, you may feel closed off from your true feelings because you're worried about "scaring" the other off. If you can be clear about how you feel, then you will know early on if you have a chance with the person, you have your eye on; and if you don't have a chance you will know to move on.

Sometimes you may get attached to a person that is just stringing you a long because you fulfil some of their needs, be it sex, financial or even both. They have no intention of committing to you and some have others they have on the side too. "Players!"

If you really like someone more than they like you, then it is important to weed them out early on to protect yourself. You need to make it clear what it is you want and lay down strict boundaries.

There are men out there that have helped me massively on my journey. I knew they liked me a lot and they knew they liked me a lot more than how I felt in return, but it didn't stop them not being afraid to be in the friend zone with me and spend their money on me, taking me out places with my son, and one even took me on an expensive holiday.

Spending time with him was massively healing. I still felt afraid to open up to my feelings because of my show hate when I am shown love, and showing love when I am shown hate, issue. I never showed hate but being closed off from your feelings and not feeling fully is not loving. Being able to really feel all your emotions is a loving experience, not only for your own self release but for others around you. The truth is beautiful and so are your emotions.

I always felt bad and guilty about it, and I did communicate it to him sometimes and he always reassured me it was fine.

My bad feelings and guilt took me away from really being able to enjoy each moment with him, but I also still had a lot of fear. I felt like I owed him something. These were super important interactions for me on my journey into love.

Some men are super sweet and super grateful just to have the company of a woman. Find these men, and if you happen to be one, let your male ego take pride in knowing you're doing a great thing for her which in turn is great for the world. Don't let your male ego feel bad and possessive over her.

How do you feel your feelings?

The simple answer is you practice. I learnt this tool from an amazing relationship coach, Rori Raye.

In the comfort of your own home, find a chair or a wall that can feel secure and stable to you. The wall or chair isn't going anywhere, it is there for you to lean on or sit on when you want. It is secure.

Feel safe and stable with the sturdy wall or the chair. Shake your body out first, really let yourself go. No one is watching you. You're safe. If people watching, get them to join in. It is important that you feel safe though. Stay present. Be aware of any feelings or sensations going on in your body. How your clothes feel against your skin.

Relax and just let go and surrender. Feel vulnerable and melt into yourself. Give yourself up to the chair or the wall.You can find a flower or something soft, feminine, and silky. Or even a spiky hairbrush. Brush it over your skin, feel open and vulnerable, really feel it and say the words out loud, while feeling it.

"I feel silky soft petals against my skin."

Sex: Good or Bad?

"I feel a cold sensation from this silky material."

"Ooo, I feel sharp prickles. Ooo that was a shock."

Practice with anything you find but be conscious and aware of your feelings from the vulnerable place I described earlier. When you realise, you're safe to be open and vulnerable with your heart open, you can then go out and practice with real people.Start with someone you see as mediocre. Someone you wouldn't care if they turned around and laughed at you or took the mickey out of you. You're doing this for you. When you see it works and you see the magic happen, you will feel comfortable doing it on more occasions,increasingly with people you do care about and then it will just feel completely natural for you to do.

If you have a habit of trusting the wrong people, then be very cautious with this and stay aware. Don't get too close to someone until they have proven to you, they care about your vulnerable feelings.

Get into the habit of saying "I feel..." You must be aware of those feelings you feel and allow them to be there. Let the feeling take over when you say it. Saying it from a closed heart won't have the same effect. If saying "I feel..." becomes a habit and you no longer feel open and vulnerable saying it, find something else to open you up. Something scary. Feel it and say it.

You could be standing in line at a coffee shop, "I am feeling flustered/tired/ bored waiting all this time." You don't always need to say "I feel..." that is just to teach yourself what you feel is ok and valid and worth expressing as you feel it authentically, any negative feelings get dispersed. But you must always be expressive. If you see something you love, get excited and say it. "That flower is so pretty!" Feel the excitement as you say it.

If you're passionate about something, talk about it. It is much more acceptable for women to be like this but if you're a man, you can do these things too, women will respond strongly as well. It just takes practice.

Anything that doesn't feel good say it!

This is a harder one and needs to be practised a lot more. If you don't feel good around your significant other, make sure you express it. But also, if you don't feel good around them and they don't seem to care, make sure you end things quickly with them as the more you see them the harder it will be to let them down. I know many men and women are afraid, especially women, and if that is you, then you need to practise standing up for yourself in their presence and saying exactly how you feel.

It can be scary, telling someone you like that you're not happy with something they did you didn't like. It can be scary saying your exact thoughts, but that is you and your truth. You must always stay true to yourself. They will be more intrigued and into you; especially if they're used to others pleasing or sucking up to them, afraid to put a foot wrong because they want love. Doing this subconsciously tells them, you're incapable of loving yourself and you are looking to drain all his love and resources.

If someone doesn't like your truth… you know there will be a man or lady out there that can and will accept you fully. You will be surprised to find that; many can handle it. If they can't or you can't, you should be avoiding them anyway. We all need a partner we can be fully ourselves around, with no fear of any authentic expression.

Sex

The tools I mention work incredibly well while having sex. Especially for a woman. Know you're worthy of great feelings and communicate exactly what you want from your partner. You love each other and want to make each other feel good. Get into feeling in the present moment. Feel from your heart and soul; your body is just a tool to heighten the feeling.

Many people have sex and focus on the end result, orgasm. To truly connect you need to feel each other's essence in the moment. In my experience, sex-addicted men can come when the woman feels able to surrender. I am guessing none of the women in porn feel able to surrender, connect to their inner essence. I have done it before. The man seems to go on for ages, and only when I am aware, I stop and melt into submission, feminine essence, thinking about God, is he able to finally have an orgasm.

CHAPTER 4

Do men only want sex?

There is a common phrase that is often said, "men only want sex" this can seem to be true if you're a woman that has experienced a lot of disappointment in your relationships with men. Men are visual creatures. They do like looking at a beautiful woman that does her best to look good, but it is not just how a woman looks or dresses, it is also how she feels in what she wears.

She can be scruffy and unkempt but if she is wearing revealing clothes to show a good body and feels good in her body, he will turn his head.

When a man is in love with a woman, he may still look at another woman, it is in his nature to do so, but if you have him emotionally connected to you, he will be very loyal. Men are very loyal when they are 100% committed to a woman. You just need to know how to get them committed. (The crucial thing you must know, is trusting that you know this information, and feeling secure in your own self and not being reliant on your happiness coming from your partner being loyal to you. Insecurity is a very unattractive trait and pushes the other away.)

Knowing that he is visual means you can dress up and look sexy just for him. It will make you feel super sexy, and he will be super happy. Men are also hunters, so if a woman looks good it is in his nature to want to hunt her down and approach her, especially if she gives off any signals that he might have a chance. Yes, he does want sex with her but it is not what he only wants. He is just following his instincts.

Men want love and relationships too and women, you can entice them to commit and give you what you want, using the tools and knowledge in this book. Men have egos and a part of that is being successful in their hunt. They watch porn because of their ego's, they are imagining they are the man, and it has nothing to do with watching the sexy woman with a good body. Yes, they are visual, but every woman can make herself look good. It is about him and his ego.

Men are initially attracted to feminine women, stereotypical feminine is laid back, soft, gentle, and vulnerable. It is important for her to feel secure and safe so she able to be this way.

You don't always have to be completely laid back. Once you have enticed him in you can be strong and have a backbone too. Men are attracted to the feminine with strong boundaries because it shows she can protect herself from other men that may try it on with her in the future if she is to become his one and only woman, but also that he won't be able to hurt her because most men, the good ones, they don't actually want to hurt you.

You need to have high boundaries that a man needs to work hard to get over, like no phone calls past a certain time because you like to get rest and sleep. Be strong. Tell him you're not cooking for a man ever again unless you're married. Have obstacles (real ones) he needs to get over to reach you. Don't be too easy and available for him with your time.

Keep yourself busy by doing things you love, don't pretend to be busy to "play the game". Focus on you and staying in your own lane, that will make him eager to join you.

Once he is over your high wall; he will have invested so much that he doesn't want to climb back over. Easy over a low wall, easy back over the low wall. If you are a woman, you are already feminine. You don't have to try to be feminine, you just need to unlearn all the masks that you built to protect yourself.

Do men only want sex?

A lot of men will have sex with any woman, if they think it is easily available to them. The men that do that don't think about the negative consequences it will have on the woman or even themselves as a man. They are just following their natural instincts. It's their nature. They are designed to enjoy naked women and to need sex. They create millions of sperm, and they need to release them.

There are women out there, who think that because they have been on a certain number of dates with a man that he paid for, they can then allow themselves to have sex with the man. I used to be one of them. It caused me heart ache and pain. I would act "cool" because being needy and clingy with a man would push him away. Deep down I was so desperate for him, but I was unable to express my feelings. I thought my feelings were "crazy" and "stupid" I didn't think my feelings were worthy of being valued. I stuffed them all down. I thought if I was smiley and happy with a man, made him dinner and gave him sex, then I would get the love I knew I deserved.

After reading many books and learning from relationship coaches, I realised that was not the case and that would never be the case. I read a few psychology books and all articles I could get my hands on to understand men. I learnt that men, connect to a woman through sex. They connect to a woman and that is why they need it so badly. As women, we are desperately needed by our men. They need us. We desperately need to heal ourselves from past traumas and feel safe in the presence of good men.

We can blame them all we want but with false information, many times (not all) we have chosen to do the actions that led us to feel pain. What men desperately desire and need more than anything else, just like women and people of all genders is love and connection. How they connect with a woman is through sex. That is how they feel loved. Men get a bad reputation for wanting to have sex with women even though they are designed to enjoy naked women and they were created that way. It is their ultimate release, and they create millions of sperm to be released. It is nature. We can't resist nature. Instead of men being hated and blamed, they need love, care, patience and understanding. They need women to be able to look after themselves and know what it is she wants so they can communicate it to them.

Men will always be attracted to a beautiful-looking woman and if they want sex they may go after her for that if it has been a while since their last release with a woman. If the woman doesn't understand him, she may think like I used to, he likes her for more. She may be flattered; she may have even purposely made herself look good to attract a man's attention. The man looking for just sex will know the woman that made herself look like she wanted to attract that. He is just following his instincts and giving her what she is giving off what she wants. So, in a way, he can tell himself he is doing good, even if at his core he feels bad.

Men do feel bad for their sexual desires, but it is their nature. What men crave above sex, is to be desired which makes them feel loved and connected.

A woman needs to love and connect to herself at the deepest part so the man can connect there and feel safe. A woman needs to feel safe, so she is able to open up and be vulnerable and be free in her feminine. She needs to feel and express everything she feels authentically in every moment. Practice makes perfect and men love it as it then makes them feel safe. I explain how you can access your feelings in the "Feelings" chapter.

However, it is a two-way street. How can a woman feel safe if she is afraid and men don't understand and don't do the necessary things to make her feel safe, so she is able to open up and feel good and comfortable in her own skin? Men desperately need the core of a woman. The feminine part of her. Women need to understand more than men what they need and do the work so that men can get what they need much more than sex. A deep long-lasting love and connection to the feminine. A woman that can really be in-tune and feel all her feelings is the ultimate magnet for a man, regardless of what she looks like.

Freedom

A lot of men value freedom above most things. A woman that feels free in being herself and feeling everything in each moment at the depth of her core will be so mesmerising, because she is free, the man will feel free. If a woman is worrying about how she looks she won't feel free. She can even feel awkward which in turn makes the man uncomfortable.

I think a lot of men stuck in their ego maybe attracted to a woman like this, also because they want to trap her and possess her. Hold her down. However, if he is able to do that, he will then struggle in the relationship, as the reason he was so attracted to her, was the fact she felt free.

A man can make a lot of effort to try and make a woman feel comfortable, but she can sometimes be closed off and afraid. If a woman feels like this, she can explain to the man,

"I feel so awkward and not comfortable, it isn't anything to do with you, but I am just not relaxed at the moment. I have a lot of fear in me from past men and you just being here and showing me what a kind, sweet, patient guy you are is really helping."

The woman can instantly feel a lot better then. She has communicated how she genuinely feels and at the same time given the man a compliment. Everyone loves a compliment, even a man. Men don't get many compliments. Give it with an open genuine heart and not to get something in return. Not even the long-term expectation of being together in a relationship.

Men other than sex want to feel like the hero. (This is the ego though). He wants to feel safe to be the protector and the provider... for a man to feel safe to do so, the woman needs to feel safe to be open and vulnerable. Men are afraid after having bad experiences with women providing for her and investing in her financially for her to then be left. They feel used.

I learnt from Renee Wade that a man being used for money gives him the same feeling that a woman gets for being used for sex. Not always but generally.

Respect

What is also extremely important to a man to feel loved is respect. Respect is the same to a man other than love. However, how is a woman supposed to respect him if he is toxic, hasn't worked on himself and doesn't respect her? There are many men that don't respect women, and this is fascinating when you learn that even more important to a man other than love is respect. They don't know the difference.

This is confusing to learn when you know what all humans really want is love and respect. Looking deeper into it they haven't learnt it themselves and perhaps somewhere inside of them they don't feel worthy of it.

Some men are not just using you for you sex. A man may really like you. If you really like him, tell him how you feel. If they are not using you, you will both know. If he is you can get rid of him. Don't wait around hoping he may one day give you a relationship. Men do NOT work like that ever. If you can't un-attach from him, make sure you date other men.

To get a man addicted to you sexually, learn to talk dirty in the bedroom. You can do it in a feminine feel-good way, but men with big egos will become addicted if you can learn to talk dirty to them. I speak more about the ego in another chapter.

CHAPTER 5

Toxic

It may not be easy for you to read but everyone has something toxic in them somewhere, even you, who is reading this book. If you hadn't then you wouldn't be reading this book. You would already be in a long, loving, and successful relationship with no experience of heart ache and without any confusion of the opposite sex, or confusion about what you might possibly be doing wrong to keep continuing the cycle of toxic relationships (if you have been).

What is Toxic?

Toxic is when you have an experience that your mind judges as a negative experience. It could have been triggered by a past event, minor or huge, and then projects that negative experience onto the other, resulting in the other retaliating negatively to you, each blaming the other for their negative experience.

For example, one spouse does something minor that is innocent, but the other spouse has a memory from the past of something similar that happened to be negative, (or they don't understand the opposite sex and it triggers them negatively, or they expect something from their spouse that they won't give) and they then blame their present spouse for the something that wasn't intentionally hurtful. The other spouse then gets triggered by feeling attacked, and an argument between the two arises.

If we can all be aware that everyone suffers and feels pain

from past traumas, then we can be more aware and loving in relationships. Instead of letting yourself go unconscious and taking the negative trigger from the other personally, realise they are reacting from their own pain and it has nothing to do with you. This way you can be more aware of how you react to it. You can come from a place of pure compassion and love for them.

If you experience abuse, allowing it to continue is toxic.

Toxic behaviours

The most obvious toxic behaviours include lying, cheating, name-calling, violence, letting your anger get out of control, manipulating and addictions. The underlying reason people use toxic behaviours is fear. It is a fear of not being loved and not knowing they're already loved by the source of creation, or some may call it "God". If you have no belief in a higher power, then believe in the love you already have within for others.

Love yourself from that place, before trying to be loved by someone else. Instead of wanting to take love, aim to give love. When you feel loved by the source of creation you know it is eternal and abundant and giving it freely feels beautiful.

Subtle toxic behaviours include, not listening, ignoring, doing something your partner asked you not to and pushing past their boundaries and not appreciating or being aware of the work your partner puts in to make you happy.

Desperately wanting something is toxic too. Desperately wanting sex, or desperately wanting a relationship, or even money in some cases. Being desperate can lead to lying or manipulation and this is toxic. Feeling desperate means, you don't believe you can get it or are worthy of it, this is toxic too.

You will find that most toxic behaviours, if not all, have a negative effect not only on the person on the receiving end but also on the person behaving in that way, but often many others too, like a domino effect.

I am going to use an extreme example using the first word of the title of this book; a woman that goes out and has sex with many different men, doesn't realise that not only is she preventing herself from being able to connect on a deeper level with a man, but she is teaching the men how to behave and unconsciously the men may expect the same from other women he encounters.

A man that goes out using and having sex with many different women doesn't realise that he is preventing himself from being able to connect deeper with a woman to the part he desperately craves and seeks. He is also damaging the woman and making her view men badly, preventing her from feeling safe with men she meets in the future. Feeling safe is extremely important for a woman so that the man can get what he desperately needs.

The following statement is true - "If you can't be happy alone, you can't be happy with another."

Many lonely and single people would love to find a man or woman to have a relationship with. Sometimes they find one and they put their happiness on the external person, and when the external person lets them down, they then blame the person for their misery.

Blaming anyone for the way we feel is toxic. Even happiness. Enlightenment is a natural state of euphoria. Nothing external creates it. However, when I believed I became enlightened, and I enjoyed my own company, I soon realised I wanted to share that happiness with someone else. Deep down, where unprocessed pain lay dormant, I desperately wanted to find the "one." I knew he was out there somewhere, but I became miserable because with every man I dated; I would find a reason why we couldn't be together. He wasn't enlightened enough. There was something toxic about him. If I looked deeper, there was something toxic in me.

I was extremely cautious and aware of "red flags" because I had been in so many other toxic situations and I was afraid to let my guard down. Also, I was educated on abusive and controlling men, and what to look out for and I didn't want to be controlled or used again. Anything small I would view it as a red flag, to keep away or I was waiting to see the red flag. And because I was familiar with abusive men, I allowed the cycle to continue with the one that manipulated me into believing he wasn't capable of harm.

Gratefully, I eventually realised that "what we see in others is a reflection of ourselves." I went deeper into myself and found what it was in me that I saw in them. It wasn't an easy journey to accept but well worth it. I couldn't love and accept it in another if I couldn't love and accept it in myself.

I remember looking at my husband in the early stages, looking at his actions that I didn't like and then realising that he must have been very spoiled. I found it off putting but when I looked deeper at myself, I discovered that, I was told I was spoiled by others while growing up and I repressed it trying to be a decent human being. I realised I didn't like it or accept it in him because I didn't like it in myself. My husband spoils me, and I am lucky to have him. I accept it myself now. My husband has always shown me love even when I act "spoiled".

He also liked to sleep a lot in his spare time, which I didn't find attractive. However, I kept meeting him and I eventually saw that he loved me even when I did those unattractive things. My ego wanted someone more energetic, so I could be more energetic, I realised that I needed love and to allow it in. He gave me love even when I believed I was unlovable.

What else is toxic?

Not being able to express your true authentic feelings is toxic because you will have them build up inside and eventually you will explode or express the feelings in other ways that are toxic. Or not expressing your true feelings to another because of fear of rejection either makes you carry on not knowing where you stand with another feeling used, or it makes you continue looking elsewhere for love, potentially ruining the connection you could have and hurting someone when they may feel the same way about you.

Feeling loved and accepted by the source of creation means there is no fear to communicate your true feelings. Every man or woman has experienced something that had a negative impact on their lives and in childhood at some point. Some are much worse than others. This creates fear and disconnection, and people suffer and end up blaming others, I used to be guilty of it too but blaming doesn't help us in our lives, it gives away the power we all have in the present moment.

If something or someone does something that triggers the unprocessed pain we experienced, or our partner does something we were taught isn't acceptable, our egos, the part of us that likes to be separate, sees conflict and pain, (in some very unconscious people, they enjoy conflict and pain, even if they're not realising it), it then triggers a negative response in the other person. I have a whole chapter on the ego to explain it in more detail.

The core of what every human needs more than anything is love and acceptance and the need to belong. Humans create this with other humans, usually in a family but if that isn't able to happen then either they create it in a group of close friendships or seek out romantic relationships.

First love and acceptance need to happen deep within ourselves. Then we can truly do it with another. Some people find that deep connection with themselves by first finding what some call God.

Past toxic experiences

It doesn't matter what level of toxic behaviour you experience from another, severe or minor, it affects future experiences in relationships.

Whether you are acting in the most toxic way or a person you were in a relationship subjected you to it; it all affects your future experiences. In my personal experience, my toxic behaviour led me into experiencing the severe toxic people that I did. It wasn't easy but we have to take responsibility for our actions and let the ego frazzle and disappear. (More explanation in the chapter "Ego").

The toxic people that I encountered led me to have a deep sense of fear of even healthy, kind men. Some of these men were still a bit toxic though, considering the route I met them and how we first started to come around; but like I said in the beginning, everyone has something toxic in them somewhere. (We can dissipate the toxic in others by being honest about our own toxicity and taking responsibility for that).

Even if I met a man that showed me love and made me feel love, I had a deep fear surrounding it and it felt like something was wrong. It was not my normal experience. Normal and familiar to me was abuse. Human nature is to like things that are familiar to us. It may have been various levels, but it was all abuse. The ego doesn't like real love. The ego desperately wants love and does all kinds of toxic things to get the love, but when it comes to real love, it is afraid.

Prevent yourself from being toxic

I mentioned earlier that not expressing your feelings is toxic. By not being present with your partner, open and there.

A man or woman can be extremely hard working and then after work wants to shut themselves off and distract themselves. Instead of being aware of their partner's presence, they're focussing on trying to de-stress, watch T.V or sleep. Being aware and grateful for your partner's presence can be extremely de-stressing in itself.

How can you be aware? You first focus on your own presence. That will automatically de-stress you anywhere, and then when you feel the love for yourself, you can then feel the love for your partner; and everything just melts into love. When a man or woman is hard at work, they can become aware of their own presence and make their work instantly lighter and work from a state of flow.

If you're the one that is putting up with your partner shutting themselves off to de-stress, you can focus on your own presence and then join them in their de-stressing task. You may actually help them de-stress fully and then you can communicate your desires from a loving place and not from a place of annoyance that they don't give you any attention.

Extremely toxic confession

I used to hate all men. I went through a phase of despising all men. I couldn't have hated them completely, because I would somehow have a glimmer of hope when another man took an interest in me.

"This is it! Now this is the man for me that I will marry and have a long loving relationship with."

When that encounter with the man started giving me negative emotions, I started playing up, and then it would soon go down the drain and I would despise men again and choose to be single for a long time and wanted to wait until the right man came along, to treat me how I deserved to be treated.

I was miserable and lonely. I would tell myself I was happy, and I would manage to get to a happy place and then I would let another man in to hurt and humiliate me. Some of them were very toxic and others were not so toxic. I learnt that I was toxic. My toxic behaviour was allowing them to treat me in certain ways and loving them, anyway, pining for them. Thinking I was a "victim," and they were terrible. Some of them were terrible. Some of them could have been given the label "Narcissist."

The film director I mentioned in other chapters, used the boiling frog method on me to keep me hooked on him. (A frog in cold water on a stove won't jump out when it gets hot, it does not realise it is in danger and instead it will allow itself to be boiled.) He gaslit me. When he left my life that is when I did loads of research on Narcissists and gaslighting. I was in awe of my discovery and what had been happening to me. I believed he did terrible things, but it was so crazy, I couldn't really believe it and made excuses for it.

This was toxic! Refusing to believe the reality because I was desperate to have a loving relationship. I couldn't believe a person could be so cruel. There are people in this world that are very un-conscious and act in very cruel ways. Some of them even disguise themselves as being conscious. To get caught up in such cruelty, I was unconscious and toxic. Allowing cruelty to continue is toxic.

More examples...

When a woman feels comfortable being friendly with another man in-front of her man, even hugging the other man farewell, he perceives it as flirting. Then instead of him expressing his feelings and trusting that she loves him enough not to go off with another man and allowing her to comfort him with love and reassurance, he becomes grumpy and vile because he is insecure; this then spoils any connection between the couple, the woman then feels rejected and unloved and reacts in a toxic and unloving way too.

In a happy and healthy and secure relationship, the man would feel secure in himself and know that she wouldn't run off with another man. He would join her and be friendly alongside her. He would feel proud that she is with him and only him. The basis for all toxic reactions is insecurity.

Another example would be when a man departs from a wom-an and he doesn't call or message her for a few days after, she doesn't understand that he needs to get back to feeling masculine again and he will get back in-touch when he is ready. An insecure toxic reaction would be to pine for this call or text message and then not answer it, pretending to busy, or they would reply straight away in excitement and happiness, placing their happiness and excitement on the message from the man.

Pretending to be busy will never get you the man because this will never get you the man because of the insecure feeling and pretence. Either he will realise right away, or he will feel it eventually and distance himself completely.

Another reaction might be that she calls him straight away, but she is coming from a place of insecurity and a fear of communicating her true feelings, subconsciously men will pick up on this and feel turned off. A woman can feel into the fear, surrender and authentically say, "I feel nervous and silly saying this, but I miss hearing your voice, and feeling safe in your presence. If she is unable to be authentic, he will be polite, but he won't be feeling masculine. An insecure toxic woman could even call him horrible names and feel anger towards him and resentment for not calling or messaging her.

A high-value and secure woman can do whatever she pleases, and it won't matter because her focus isn't on getting a man but on feeling secure on her own, happy, and healthy. She doesn't care about a man. She cares about her own feelings and being in-control of herself. When I first learnt and understood that men need to get back to feeling masculine again, getting their testosterone back up after being with a woman, and focusing on their work and their goals, I started to be able to feel a love and respect for them, instead of a hatred and resentment that they abandoned me.

It was easy, when dating many men that I wouldn't normally choose to go out with, using them for practice. However, it could be seen as toxic using men for such things but if you're a woman in a deeply toxic place then it is definitely a step up to get practice in, practice feeling safe, seeing that there are lots of good men out there. Most men are happy to be around a lovely lady and they do not expect sex right away.

One coach I learnt a good amount from is Renee Wade, The Feminine woman. She is against circular dating as she says it prevents you from establishing a real connection with a man. I must agree with her on that. It can get tiring and you're always looking for the next man.

However, if you want to get married and a man marries you,

you can build on the connection part after feeling safe and secure that he will not abandon you. Feeling super secure and safe in yourself and who you are committing to, knowing they're fully committed back. It is a wonderful feeling. I recently saw a YouTube video where it suggested not dating more than; I think they said about 5 men at a time as you get tired and confused and then don't want to see any of them. That happened to me a few times, but I kept on trying after prolonged periods of being alone.

Toxic sex

Sex is toxic when you can't control your sexual urges and you do things that hurt yourself and others.

When I was young, I sent nude pictures of myself to men I liked hoping it would make them want me. I knew they would only want sex with me, but I believed that if they came close enough, then one might fall in love with me if I was good enough in bed.

Or a man may send nude pictures of himself, especially of his penis to a woman he has never met, making the woman he sent it to feel unsafe. He does this because he is not aware of women and how we are. He thinks to himself, "I like naked women's pictures and I love my dick! If I send pics of my dick, hopefully she will send me naked pictures back."

Of course, this usually responds to the woman blocking him. Some women that are not aware of how men are and enjoy "cheap" attention, may respond by sending back her own nude pictures. This teaches the ego driven men that it is acceptable to do as they please. Sending random photos of nude body parts is sexual harassment.

CHAPTER 6

Love Island

I remember the first time I caught a glimpse of love Island, "cringy, reality rubbish" were my initial thoughts. I had stopped watching the news because it was depressing, and not long after I stopped watching Eastenders; I realised it had the same effect of triggering me negatively with the dramatic story lines. It wasn't even real-life gossip. Fantasy gossip.

I wanted peace, love and happiness and I knew TV wasn't fulfilling. Just addictive, a distraction from the dark parts of my mind that needed addressing, not triggering, and covered over with TV, "It's just TV!" Then why was it so triggering?

I didn't know much about the story lines on Love Island, but I knew that people went on Big Brother to get a bit of fame, so I gathered it was like that.

I couldn't believe there was a reality TV game show just about love and romance. I found it disgusting that this show that caused real life feelings and emotions in people was on T.V for entertainment. I remember one year, a guy I was "seeing" (weird, either you're with someone or not!) he was addicted to Love Island and I remember being made to watch quite a few episodes back-to-back. I did start getting into it. I was horrified to learn that people couple up and then decide to either continue in that couple or go on to find a new person to couple up with. Horrifying! This was on TV for everyone to watch and it creeped me out.

"Vile and disgusting show!" I thought. Since being married to my husband, I found myself being able to watch it. I watched quite a few episodes of 2022. I guess I felt safe having my husband and being in a relationship with him, and I was able to not get triggered too much.

We watched it in the middle of me writing my book too, so I knew I was able to write about what triggered and upset me. I was able to see the couples and get more of a feel of them and what was going on, rather than watching it and rejecting it because I couldn't stand it.

The only good thing Love Island teaches is that wherever you go, whatever situation you're in, if you're single you can form a bond with someone and "couple up". Or if you're already "coupled up" it is possible to go on and want to couple up with someone else. Continuing a relationship with that person is a choice. Choosing to love someone is a choice. When you are married, you are choosing to love that person for life and only to be with them. Marriage is a symbol and a sign that you are fully committed to each other.

The Ego

The most prominent couples that I remember on Love Island 2022, were Jacques, Paige and Adam, and Tasha, and Andrew. I heard about Gemma and Luca but unfortunately, I didn't see the episode to comment on them. I heard there was a lot of misogynistic behaviour from Luca though which would have been good for me to comment on.

I will start with Jacques and Paige. Paige, as the sweet feminine woman she is, believed they were in a relationship, they were coupled up, so they were in a couple. I think this is beautiful as they hadn't even had sex, I always believed once you had sex that was the unspoken rule to say you would be together in a relationship. This made me think of her as a sweet angel.

Jacques then went to Casa Amor to be tested to see if he was able to stay loyal to Paige. His excited little boy, Jack the lad came out and he was playing with two different girls in there even kissing one of them. Very egoistical. He used them for fun and even lied to them. He then chose to stay coupled up with Paige.

Of course, Paige then finds out about his actions and is absolutely heartbroken and distraught. She was angry with him and chose not to speak with him for a while. Paige was able to show her true feelings around this, she didn't bottle them up and pretend she was OK. She was real and raw. Even though it was her ego expecting them to be in a relationship and for him to behave.She didn't understand him as a man. Men will do as they please if they don't have the spoken instruction not to do something. They forget and need simple instructions for this. Have you heard the phrase "men are not mind readers"? If you understand this, then you will realise that it is fine for you as a woman to do the same. If Paige understood him as a man, she could have verbalised what she expected from him before he went to Casa Armor.

When Jacques responded to Paige, he even tried to justify his actions and said, "We're both single!" This enraged Paige's ego even more and she was terribly upset. Her ego was dented thinking that she and Jacques had something going together and seeing that he didn't think the same.

When Jacques realised that he hurt Paige deeply he then opened his heart out to make it up to her. This is not an easy thing to do. He even had to write it down first to read it out to her. It was too much for him to say it and feel it at the same time, opening his heart.

As a Jack the lad male with an ego around women, this would have been extremely dangerous and very daring to do. He felt safe because Paige happily showed her true feelings around his actions.

Unfortunately, the damage had been done. He ruined the connection that Paige thought they had in her head. Once the damage is done, it is not easy to go back. If you have been with someone a long time and invested a lot in them it can be done, but this pair

Sex: Good or Bad?

had only been "seeing" each other for a few weeks.

After Jacques poured his heart out publicly on national TV, he assumed they had made up. Paige said they had, and they even kissed, even though her heart had gone through pain from him; it was then her turn to be tested with Adam Collard, an extremely handsome and tall male that most of the girls melted for, including Paige.

Paige again, not understanding the fragility of the male ego, decided that she wasn't going to fuss too much about being com-pletely loyal to Jacques and she ended up getting comfortable with Adam.

Jacques's ego really couldn't handle it and he had to leave the Island. I thought it was an extremely sad moment, as a person understanding the fragility of the male ego.

I do wonder if Jacques's ego in Casa Armour showed up so strongly because he was struggling mentally. He said after leaving, he was struggling weeks before. The thing with the ego, as I will mention in the next chapter is that it doesn't like to connect. It is afraid of a loving connection. Also, some people's ego doesn't be-lieve it is worthy of love, which is why the ego feels it has to get in the way of a true loving connection. Fear.

I believe that Paige and Adam's connection wasn't real on Paige's part. She had already invested emotions with Jacques and was trying to cover her hurt of feeling disconnected with a new man and possibly show Jacques what it felt like. Revenge is never a good idea. Conscious or unconscious.

When Jacques left the show, she had no choice but to contin-ue with Adam. I think Adam was just a bit of fun for her to feel better about Jacques doing it. Again, all ego stuff and spoiling the true connection that can be made. I may be mistaken with what I saw, but that is my personal opinion on it.

Now, on to Tasha and Andrew. This was also an uncomfort-able ego reaction for me to see. I didn't see all the episodes so I can only comment on what I did see.

I think Andrew was genuinely really into Tasha and her flirting with Billy really hurt his male ego. If you read my other chapter, you see that women need to view themselves with a lot more worth because when a man hunts a woman and is successful, his ego feels so satisfied.

If another man comes along into the picture, their ego is then severely damaged, the ego then feels it has to do even more damage, to feel better.

In Andrew's case, he coupled up with Coco and even got a little bit physical with her. I think his ego just needed to know he could get with another woman and be physical. Coco didn't get Andrew to invest in her enough before getting physical with him to keep his interest in her for longer.

Getting physical is a much deeper commitment for a woman, so when Tasha learned what he did with Coco, she was furious for ages. However, if she knows how fragile the male ego was, she would have known that flirting with Billy and choosing him was a big mistake. Some egos' even get violent and so jealous, even when there is no need or even any evidence of cheating.

Some male egos can't even handle a woman talking to another man, and if she gives a platonic hug, hell can be let loose. If you're a man reading this, it is so important to know that when woman is comfortable chatting to another man in your presence, usually it is that she is super happy and comfortable with you, to be able to do that. She feels safe because you're nearby.

For Tasha to go off and flirt with Billy, I think Tasha felt fear from Andrew's deep genuine likeness towards her, she just wanted to see his reaction to her feeling free with Billy.

The fact he reacted by getting close to Coco, showed her ego, he didn't care that much. She wanted him again.

Some women have a deep-rooted fear, and some may test

the man she is with to see if he is the jealous violent type. The fear is also the fear of connecting deeply because of connecting to an abusive man in the past.

The ego likes to prevent connections and remembers' past pain. Like the domino effect I mentioned in the previous chapter, the male ego abusing a woman, hurts her and she then needs to protect herself from future men. She is even afraid of good-hearted gentlemen.

The toxic ego gets what it is set out to do. Continues the pattern of pain and torment in people's lives.

CHAPTER 7

Ego

This chapter may be difficult to read as it exposes the ego, and the ego doesn't like to be exposed. Do try to get through it until the end though.

What is ego?

The most important thing we need to know about the ego is that it damages the loving connection we want to create with others. The ego is the part of us that thinks it is separate from others.

Examples of ego thinking include, "I am better than them" or "I want to be the best" or "I am a victim, in pain and no one understands" or "those people understand, lets group together" or in Eckhart Tolle's simple words, the ego is an identity. Eckhart is aware that his identity is now a "spiritual teacher."

The ego creates suffering, when it has been deflated, it hurts. In extreme cases it enjoys creating suffering in others because of the personal pain it has been through. The ego is revengeful and likes to get revenge. "You hurt me, so I will hurt you!" Some egos believe that others are out to cause them pain and are extremely guarded. The ego can also feel threatened in someone else's presence, and for no reason it creates drama and negativity.

The ego wants

The ego wants love and to feel loved, it acknowledges power

as being loved. It is unaware that your true self is pure essence, and you are already the purest form of love, and already intently powerful. Because of the egos' lack of awareness, it is the cause of anything toxic.

Whenever it feels its power being taken away, it reacts. The ego can get in the way when a disagreement is present or when it doesn't get what it wants.

Some people know their true selves are pure essence and in love and can connect to their true selves, but then their ego takes over and instead of feeling it and connecting to it, they are knowing it; that knowing is from the head, thoughts and it then comes from the ego.

The ego wants to be right more than it wants love. If you find yourself in an argument with your partner and they cannot let go of and accept you have a different opinion, ask them if they care more about having a loving relationship or care more about being right.

It is extremely hard in a relationship even if you think you're enlightened. When you are easily triggered it is a sign that you have unconsciously let the ego take control. In some circumstances the ego may accept bad behaviour because it wants to feel superior by not retaliating. However, letting someone treat you badly is not good or loving for the other person. It just lets their ugly ego grow.

The "I am a victim" ego identity is used to being treated badly, and is comfortable with familiarity, so it ends up repeating the cycle. They may believe they are acting lovingly to the other, but they are not. "What we do to others we do to ourselves" So allowing someone to treat you badly is not good for them and their connection to their true loving selves.

Judging the opposite sex

The ego will often judge others by how they talk, dress, do their hair, and or make-up.

The ego likes to judge people's actions and think they are better than the other because they are not like that. However, we all need to remember "what we see in others is a reflection of ourselves!" When you allow your ego to judge others, you're not seeing their perfect inner essence and you are certainly not connecting to your own.

Wanting Revenge

When the ego feels damaged or hurt it can want to get revenge on the person that hurt it. It can't let it go or take any responsibility for its own actions that may have caused it. I used to feel anger and resentment against guys using me for sex. I felt hurt because I wanted them and felt they should have known better.

They did know better. They were as bad as I thought of them to be but my longing for love always let them come over repeatedly. I realise now that they were just men and getting what they needed from me easily. They probably did feel unbelievably bad about it, but they couldn't help their natural instincts. It was up to me to know what I wanted, have boundaries, and communicate them.

I used to feel angry and wanted revenge. That was my ego making me act toxic. When we do something bad to another, we are coming away from our true loving selves. Every time we do that, we're expanding the ego. The ego getting revenge damages the loving connection to their true selves, instead of being able to fully express their authentic feelings of pain they felt by the other that was on many occasions unintentional. Even if it is intentional, it is only intentional from their ego and not their true authentic selves.

The ego feels embarrassed by being damaged and the negative feelings caused, and the true person is unable to communicate their feelings.

When someone is unable to communicate their feelings, it gets bottled up. Eventually their feelings often explode in very toxic ways. By wanting to be right and judging the situation, the ego

damages the connection by again keeping separate and not connecting.

Hello Good Looking.

Nature makes it so that most people are attracted to physical
good looks. It is the ego that desperately wants a person with physical attractiveness. It is the ego that wants the good-looking person.
Nature wants us to procreate with good genes, however, it is the
ego that will continue to hunt someone down, desperately wanting
that good-looking person and not accepting "no" for an answer.

Many incredibly good-looking people's egos can get caught
up in the way they look. Narcissistic personality disorder, the name
comes from Narcissus. He was a character in Greek mythology, he
was so caught up in his own beauty that he rejected all romantic
advances and just stared at his reflection in the water until one day
he died. He never got to feel a loving connection with anyone.

The way an attractive person looks, can make others feel
a certain way and they then want to relieve themselves of their
sexual gratification. The animalistic, lizard/survival brain part of us.
When a man or woman with a big ego about their appearance,
continues to keep attracting the opposite sex, they will think their
looks are enough to keep them.

However, the belief that looks alone are good enough is huge-
ly from the ego. A woman will continuously get hurt by being used,
and a man's ego will inflate, because he can easily get a woman,
but deep down he will feel disconnected. He will blame women for
being hysterical and dramatic and the woman will blame the man
for just wanting sex.

To the ego, the best human to be with looks good and has a
comfortable bank balance. Money is power and the ego loves to
be powerful.

The ego wants success. This is the reason why men (and
women who want to be seen as equals) go out and get laid and

have their pals cheering them on.

When a man just wants to sleep with many women it is his ego bigging him up. What women need to know is if that a man's biological drive is to have sex and him doing so makes him successful, then she is the amazing prize. That is how amazing a woman is to a man. It is important for women to see this and know this about themselves because so many women have low self-esteem and don't feel good about themselves. It is also important to lessen the huge ego in men that unintentionally cause suffering in women. Women can do this by surrendering their ego first, into their authentic vulnerable selves.

Ego and Feelings

Women tend to have bigger victim mentality egos. As a woman, with this victim mentality, I had to do a lot of self-analysis and face uncomfortable feelings to get out of this mentality. Facing the uncomfortable feelings was also frazzling the ego and letting it dissipate.

I use the word "frazzle" a lot because that is what it can feel like to the ego. It is a burning up of the ego, to get it to dissipate. If you are able to do this, you will feel uncomfortable but if you can allow it, you will notice you are just the watcher of the ego that is being "frazzled".

It is hard for the male ego to hear this, but many men do tend to have bigger egos than women, when it comes to power and control. Women have higher painbodies. Please read Eckhart Tolle, "The Power of Now".

An ego is also the part that feels uncomfortable, negative and victimised around people judged to be more powerful than them. If you see someone as having an ego, that too is your own ego. "What we see in others is a reflection of ourselves."

When a man feels he has a chance (or wants a chance) with a good-looking woman, and his ego doesn't get what it wants, he can turn nasty and sometimes violent. A woman's ego can be like this after she has had sex with a man and wants a relationship with him.

If the man or woman stays connected to their true power, and true inner selves and does not react to another person's ego with theirs, just like anyone not reacting to a toxic ego, the power from staying connected to their true selves, means they will keep the other ego from getting too out of hand, keeping the situation as calm as possible with little drama. Some people are so deeply connected to their true power that their power can even help to frazzle the other person's ego in that moment.

Ego's battle with each other. True power frazzles the ego with truth.

The victim's ego is easier to diminish as its existence is pain. This is why many people that suffer can go on to be highly successful in life.

The ego doesn't want to die. The ego is the identity that the person has had for a long time. Your true self connected to what many call God, knows that it's love never dies.

Ego Switch

The ego can switch. If in power and then affected by a challenge, the ego can then feel victimised. Some victimised egos can even turn violent, to try and gain a level of power. I have witnessed and experienced being able to frazzle men's and women's egos, by accessing my own true inner self. It isn't always painful for their ego as they're in the presence of true love, true power. On occasions when it is painful, they don't react negatively as they know they are not being judged, only loved.

If someone has flashes of connecting to their true power around someone with narcissistic personality disorder, the person with narcistic personality disorder will have flashes of pure terror. The person with flashes of connection to their true power, will be afraid of their true power because of the terror they sense from the narcissist.

They are with the narcissist because they are afraid of their own true power, that is why they get sucked back in to yet another abusive relationship, familiar with what they already know.

When people fall in love; for a certain amount of time their ego has been silenced. The ego got what it wanted. The ego is never satisfied for long though.

The ego comes back into action destroying any connection made when it is no longer being made happy by the other person. When the person they fell in love with stops doing what they did, or the honeymoon period is over, and they start to see annoying habits they didn't see before, they can end up arguing and eventually their relationship will be destroyed.

Like I said before, many men are not going to like to acknowledge it, but many tend to have much bigger egos than women. A woman to a man is a weakness, a weakness to his ego. If it goes wrong when he lets his ego drop for a woman, in the future, it is going to be much worse for other women he encounters. Just like women, too, when anyone experiences pain when we let our guard down, we're less likely to let it down again. Some men, not all men, lie to get a woman into bed.

Ego in Bed

When a man gets a woman gets into bed with him, the man has managed to get her to let her guard down. (Unless she chose to do it for some other reason). She has usually totally surrendered her ego. The man on the other hand, has only inflated his ego even more, unless she got a commitment from him first. (She needs to learn to totally surrender her ego to herself and communicate what she really wants from him beforehand.)

Good men, bad men, ALL men feel a deflated ego if they're rejected by a woman. It is never easy for a man to be forward to a woman. The male ego can sometimes react very badly to rejection. Understanding and compassion are important. If you're a man maybe this has been you one time or maybe it will be in the future. Instead of feeling bad, feel like you're brave and courageous for asking and being vulnerable sharing your feelings.

A woman can keep herself safe by responding by talking to his ego. "I am very impressed that you asked me, and I am flattered too but I am not available at this time." She could also lie and say she has a partner already. Unfortunately too many men's ego's are dangerous and sometimes the only way a woman can be safe is to massage his ego.

You can be in a loving relationship with someone that your ego doesn't perceive as looking good and with someone that you think (your ego judges) isn't great, (I use the word think, Rene Descarte philosophy was "I think, therefore I am. Eckhart Tolle actually discovered the truth, "I am therefore I think".

Before we can think, we must first be alive. Being alive is always in the present moment and we use "I am" in the present moment.

Thinking is a doing word and something that we do and if we can be aware of the ego, we can learn to control our thoughts. ("I am", is being and we're already doing that without doing anything or even thinking.)

So, when you think a person isn't great, by looking at their actions and the way that they think, that is your ego judging them, those are your thoughts about them.

If that person's actions and thoughts are loving towards you, it is feasible to develop a loving relationship with them, if you focus on the good things they do for you.

You have to see their core essence. The core essence, which is in every being and in yourself. You must realise that when you think "they're not great", it's your judging ego. If you continue to be with someone you think isn't great, you will only suffer.

Either make a conscious decision not to be with them or tap into your own inner essence. Your own inner love. It is a beautiful place to

Ego

be. When you tap into your inner love, you will see the love within the other person.

Before knowing what, I know now, I met with a man that I wasn't particularly interested in. I had my fear up, the ego that wants to be right. It prevented me from being able to connect at the loving place deep within or acknowledge the sweet gestures from this man, as it was comparing him to the past men, who had caused me tremendous pain. I learnt that it was far safer and more loving to be with someone who genuinely loves me.I realised that my traumatised pain body and my ego, would have continued if I didn't acknowledge this. My pain body (Eckhart Tolle explains in more detail what this is in his book, "The Power of Now") and my ego would match love with hate and hate with love.

If someone showed me love, I would not be as loving as I should be, I would think there was something wrong with them and if someone showed me hate, I would have to match it with love. The pain I endured by loving someone that showed me hate was immense. Letting a man use me for sex, was a type of hate. I longed and longed for the man to show me love in return and would wait and hope that he would miraculously be more loving and show me love and give me the relationship I knew I deserved.

The ego won't like to acknowledge that, as the individual it must learn about the opposite sex. The ego always likes to blame and never takes responsibility. A woman will be dramatic because of the past hurt she has felt and not processed understanding the man. The pain body will arise and instead of accepting and under-standing it, blame is the first thing.

A man is a man. He is programmed in his DNA to want sex and to release his sperm. He will do that if given the chance. It is also seen as being macho by his friends and a very egotistical thing to do as well. Ego's like to encourage other ego's rather than speak the truth.

Men and women need to learn about each other so they can love each other and respect each other. The ego is only concerned with itself, but it is important for the entire planet to end the conflicts within, to stop wars happening in the outside world.

Women and some men often say if a woman ruled the world there would be no wars. Well, what if I told you that women have this power already, without taking away a man's egoistical power?

However, I am learning to be less afraid of people and more grounded in myself the more I surround myself with mostly good people, and I spend less time with people with severely toxic egos. I am learning to be less afraid of people and more grounded in myself. You can use the fear, which is ego, and surrender it, when with the opposite sex. When I first used to go on dates, I used to be so quiet and so shy, and I never used to speak. I thought I am pretty, one of these guys will stick around. Sometimes they did but I wasn't attracted to them.

Many took advantage of me and got sex from me. They could sense my vulnerability and would try their luck to see what they could get away with. I would freeze in fear. I don't think they knew I was in fear, as their manly ego was focused on getting a beautiful young lady.

I was often scared and quiet but not confident. When I started learning about feminine energy and vulnerability, I realised I already naturally emitted it strongly. That is why I would easily attract them. I started to learn to use it differently.

My realisation of how I hated men using me, caused me to practise being bold and outgoing. I started to try to take control of the situation, however I still didn't really have control of the situation. I would put up a bit of a fight, but their fight was often stronger than mine. After a while, it was easier to give in than to not, and sometimes I would freeze in fear again.

Porn Egos

By taking control I would push past the fear and just be good at it. I guess that is what porn stars do. They're afraid but they push past their fear and put on an act. Which is sad. Especially when you know the reason why men watch porn. Men watch porn for their egos. They don't care about the woman. They are visual and enjoy looking, but they get off by imagining they are the man. When a woman is secure in a man's love, it is fine to use this knowledge to have some fun between you. But as the whole planet's consciousness shifts higher, eventually in relationships, sex will be intimate, loving and purely for connecting. Karma Sutra, tantric, no means to an end goal, which is orgasm.

When you know the reason for Eckhart Tolle's work and the necessity to frazzle the ego and the pain body, it is sad that porn is still being made. The women and men in the videos will all have high pain bodies and the watchers also have a pain body, trying to escape it. Like a drug, just causing more pain. "What we see in others is a reflection of ourselves." If you see the opposite sex as having such a massive ego, then it is likely you need to look at yourself more deeply. The ego hates being exposed. The ego has to always be right. The ego can't stand taking any responsibility. When you realise that you are not the ego, it can make it easier. You can then watch it frazzle in pain. An ego death.

Toxic Ego Affirmations

A very toxic man's ego will easily be dented. You can have the stereotypical macho violent man, or you can have the financially successful man. Knowing that the ego likes to be right, the toxic ego affirmation can be "I am unsuccessful with the opposite sex" which prevents you from trying and only repeating the cycles from the past. It can even be "they only want me for my money!" Or "they only want me for my looks!"

It may be true with some members of the opposite sex, but if you see that as coming from their ego and not their loving soul self, you can then feel better by being in your own soul self and therefore helping them tune into their own soul self. Soul self can also be described as essence, the deep part that is love, joy and freedom.

When you can be in your own loving soul essence, you see it in other's and then help them to connect to that part of themselves.

Anger is toxic and is created by the ego. Even though at times, it is important to express anger in a healthy and non-destructive way. If we are not aware of our anger, we can lose control and it can take us away from the loving and connecting feelings we want to create with our significant other.

Women more than men often repress their anger as they are afraid to disconnect from their partner and "scare him away" if they're not nice or good enough. This then boils up and they let their anger out in dramatic and unhealthy ways later. Many women don't realise that most men want to please their woman and keep them happy. Expressing your true feelings of anger exactly when it arises can be a way to connect and feel love with your partner when you see he wants the opportunity to be the hero and to make it better.

Men want to be the hero. We all want to have a loving connection. I learnt from Rori Raye that you can say,

"I feel angry when... and I don't like feeling that way! I don't know what to do, what do you suggest?"

Or if a man shows up and he is late you can say, "I feel confused, I am happy to see you, but I feel angry that you're late." It is not easy. With a lot of practice you will prevent future drama and situations blowing up in angry ways.

Men, now you know this, try to not react by letting your own ego be triggered. Instead realise that her angry outburst was her repressing her anger for a while because she didn't want to create any drama.

Anger comes from the pain and frustration of not being listened to, and not feeling respected. When we know these simple things, we can start to practise really listening to our partners. Many men don't realise that when a woman is complaining about something, she doesn't want to fix it, she just wants to be listened

Ego

to. Some men are the same. They don't want to fix things in their life, they just want someone to listen so they can feel loved. Sometimes it can be the ego enjoying complaining and getting sympathy from others, as that is the only way they learned to get love.

Some people can't handle listening to some people's feelings, so they do something unintentionally called "gas lighting". They dismiss their reality. Remember, they don't want you to fix anything, they just want you to listen to them. Narcissists "gaslight" their victims on purpose, but I think many people in the world do it because they don't know how to prevent the other person from feeling badly. It makes them feel bad they can't fix it.

If this is you, all you need to do is listen and give a beautiful reassuring hug if wanted. If we can all practise keeping aware of the part of us that gets triggered and start to communicate our negative responses in a loving way, then we can avoid horrible arguments ever. If we can prevent our negative response, we can help our partner and the relationship.

When you start to practise communicating what hurts you and what you want and see that your partner stops doing the things that hurt you and does what you ask, your love will grow. Some people may see that their partner does not care to try and show them love however much they are trying their hardest to create a loving bond. The most loving thing you can do is force them to face their ego by facing yours and leaving the relationship. When you trust and have faith that what is best for you is to leave the relationship, amazing things will happen for you. Some may like to trust in God or the Universe too.

Sex: Good or Bad?

CHAPTER 8

Porn

Porn is so easily available these days. A quick google search instantly produces hundreds of images and videos. It was first produced by men for men but over the decades more and more women have got into the industry as producers.

One of my magazines contained an article written by a woman that wanted to make a porn video. She wanted to be happy and positive about the situation and create something from a woman's perspective.

I remember reading how excited she was about finding the actress/sex worker and making this porn film. While the actress-sex worker was performing she looked over to the film maker and made eye-contact, but the film maker couldn't look. The film maker felt deeply ashamed for exploiting this woman.

Porn is just visual and the only feelings you experience from it are animalistic feelings. Physical body sensations. There are no emotions or feelings involved and absolutely no feelings or emotions can be created to make a connection with another human being or even yourself or the higher power that created you.

After a heated argument about porn with a previous partner, I created this message on social media,

"If your partner suggests watching porn, agree and say "Ok, gay porn" and see how he reacts!"

I was angry and frustrated and thought my response was hilarious. I wanted my partner to acknowledge me and want to connect with me, not watch porn which has no emotional depth to it.

His reaction was entertaining though. His whole body flinched as he said, "No".

A woman commented on my post. She said that in cavemen times, when people have sex, it was a signal to others to have sex, as it was a part of nature.

Back then it was nature, animalistic, lizard survival brain, but we have evolved a lot since those days and today many people are disconnected from others. Being a part of a tribe in cavemen days is extremely different to watching a screen alone in your bedroom. Even if you're with your partner watching it, you're not connecting and bonding emotionally with your partner, which in my eyes is the most important part of sex. Feeling a soul-to-soul connection.

If a person watches a lot of porn, how will they know how they really feel when they are with another human being?

To properly connect to another human being, we first need to connect to our inner selves. Not our outward bodily selves. Porn is a visual outward body experience. You see what you see, and may copy it, believing that your partner may like that because you saw it in porn. Some may think they like it because they saw it in porn and think they're doing a good thing for themselves and their partner. In reality, there is no real connection or bonding going on.

In real life a woman and a man should both feel safe to be able to be open and communicate what they desire to their partner.

My Porn Journey

In my teenage years, I used to find porn fascinating. In my search for true love, I felt because men enjoyed porn, I had to become the woman they enjoyed watching so much. To please my man, I pushed through a lot of boundaries to try and be the best sexual woman. I mistakenly thought that it would bring me a true connection with a man. After having sex, I also assumed that I would be in a relationship but after many painful experiences, I soon realised that wasn't the case. I used to sometimes get off on porn myself, I know I used to imagine being the sexy woman wearing the sexy lingerie and then wanting to re-enact it.

My ego thought if I was sexy like that, I would capture a man. I enjoyed and loved feeling sexy. I always felt empty, unfulfilled, and sad when I didn't get the relationship I wanted. I would blame the man for only wanting sex. It was hypocritical as I had gone after that myself and was still not getting the result I really wanted. I wasn't thinking about myself past the sexy feeling stage. The physical body stages.

I had a lot of unprocessed traumata. Pushing past my boundaries, somehow made me feel less ashamed, like I was in control of and growing my self-worth. I felt like what I was doing was normal.

When going through Felicity Keiths' programme, "The Language of Desire", I found it interesting that men watch porn not for looking at the sexy women on the screen, but for their egos. They imagine they are the man in the video with the woman. They don't care too much for the woman.

So, when I dressed sexily to please a man, I also wanted to please myself thinking I looked so good a man would wed me one day. At the time I didn't realise I was on a long painful journey.

I enjoyed dressing sexily, but I needed to be in a safe relationship to avoid the trauma and pain associated with doing it outside a relationship.

When in some parts of this book I give tips to teach you to eradicate your ego to have a healthy and happy relationship, you can see what the main problem with porn is. Porn encourages the ego.

Much of my self-esteem and low self-worth issues which allowed me to accept extremely poor behaviour from men, came from constantly being tormented and bullied by an older family member. My father used the words "torture" not many years before he sadly passed away.

This older family member also sexually abused me and raped me as a child. "Eurgh! Thick sticky boys wee" I thought. It wasn't until my late teenage years that it finally clicked that it wasn't boys wee. He was only a kid himself at 13 or 14 but to me he was like an adult as I was only about 6.

This family member one day sat me down and put on 1990's or 1980's soft porn and he asked to act it out with me. "No" I whined in disgust feeling violated. We could blame the adults that left us alone together, but if porn wasn't accessible then he may never have had the ego reaction towards it and thoughts in his head to try it.

When I was 16 and heavily stoned and unconscious, a boy 17 refused to take my "no" for an answer. I wasn't in any state to fight him off and he raped me.

I wasn't intimidated by this boy and had experimented with sex with him before. This particular time, I really wasn't interested. I had said "no" to him, and he didn't take my "no" for an answer.

When I sobered up, I was angry. Dangerously angry.

I started to bully and harass him constantly to get my revenge. It made me feel powerful. One day my friend and I chased him into the public toilets. My friend squeezed his bag out from under the cubicle and we ran off with it. Surprise, surprise, inside his bag was a collection of porn magazines.

These are two separate occasions in my life where I was raped and had evidence that the perpetrator was looking at porn.

I want to add that I have always had naturally large breasts, hips with a waist, a pretty face and long hair. Nature's instinct makes most men react animalistically.

For research, I watched a documentary called "Afghanistan's Top Porn Star". The woman the documentary was about had been sexually oppressed and shamed as a child and a teenager.

She was forced to wear a hijab as a teenager and taught that sex was wrong.

Porn stars that were sexually abused as children felt a lot of shame and were oppressed as they felt too much shame and didn't feel able to tell anyone and had to carry a secret.

Both cases are from shame and oppression in childhood.

I didn't feel the need to add this, but I will because of the deeper message behind it. Before my family member that wanted to "play games" with me that was abuse and rape, a boy the same age as me aged 5 or 6 wanted to first the play the game he called "bums and willies".

He also ended up getting his friend to play too. Only when they tried to get another one of my family members to play, it was found out. She told on me and I was shouted at by my father. I was sent to my room without any dinner. I believe then, that is when the older family member found out that made me play with him.

"If they play with her, I can play with her too!" It was my very first experience of another male thinking they could have access to my body, just because I had been accessed before.

I remember the 6-year-old boy putting the film, "Dirty Dancing" on. Certified 15 rating. Copying what he witnessed at such a young age.

Interesting facts

- Most women that do porn or sell sex have been sexually abused as children, many feel desperate and have been taken advantage of and exploited. Some were even promised a good career in the industry but only used once.

Sex: Good or Bad?

- Some women are forced to do porn and perform sexual acts they are not comfortable with.

- Some porn acts are violent. Does this help a person
  connect to his true soul self, loving and accepting their
  own self and others?

Me too – The #MeToo movement has helped bring justice and closure to many women who have been sexually abused unfortunately men have also suffered major trauma from sexual abuse. Some of it may be hidden so if you or people you know have been through this harrowing experience – see someone about it or write a journal to try and unearth and help you overcome some of the self-sabotaging habits you may have developed that ultimately kill your relationships.

Porn can teach you how to physically please others. On the downside, it can frustrate you into violent and illegal acts. Porn will never teach you how to have a deep emotional and spiritual connection to keep someone you might want to spend a long part of your life journey with.

CHAPTER 9

Dating

When you first start to look for a partner ... you can date more than one at a time, but you must not expect any of them *to be the one*. Dating more than one person will stop you from losing yourself in one man or woman and pining for them.

You need to practise and practise again the feeling messages you learnt in the "Feelings" chapter and say exactly as you please to your date. So, if they do or say something you don't like, tell them (to an extent, no insults or abuse, lol!).

This is just to make you feel more confident and to see their reactions to your feelings when you express them.

When you first go on dates, you're there to have fun, get to know them, and see if you have a good time together. You're there to practise being silly and feel safe being yourself, and to see whether they are still into you and if you are still into them.

Practice being open and vulnerable with some feeling messages, see their reactions and see how your feeling messages work.

Women, you can date guys that you don't see as being "manly". Over time you will see another side. Are you there for macho, or for love and care? When we struggle to find a nice partner, we are often attracted to ones that will hurt us. We must make a conscious choice to date another type of person, so we can find a partner that won't hurt us.

Sex: Good or Bad?

Men, you can date women that you don't find attractive, you may be surprised that you start to find her attractive after getting to know her. Especially if you are in a cycle of unsuccessful relationships. It all helps in frazzling the ego.

When you are connected to your heart, you can't hurt another. You are in tune with love, you have it, you want it. You can give it to them. When we give it to a person we're infatuated over or want something from, we love in hope for it to be returned, that is conditional love.

If we find a partner that is good and nice, we can learn to find them exciting. The exciting part is finding yourself, feeling free to be yourself, finding security and stability in the love from your partner. When you stay faithful and loyal long enough to your partner, you will find the sex becomes more meaningful, deeper and loving. Women will feel safe to open up to the deeper part of themselves that the man craves, as long as he is able to make her feel safe to open up to that vulnerable part of her place.

A woman can get there independently as long as she feels surrendered connecting to the source of creation that loves us all.

Remember all the great stuff your partner adds to your life and remember all the heartache from the past!

When you choose to stay with a person for a long time, you will fall more in love with them each day you are together. This is very different from a quick rush and then it falls apart with agonising heartaches.

It is acceptable to expect the man to pay for the dates, he is the man after all. Women need to feel taken care of... in return when the man gives her exactly what she wants, she will feel safe to take care of him and his needs.

A book I read called," The Five love languages" by Gary Chapman, explains that we all have one primary love language to feel loved and if we don't have our love language fulfilled, we will not feel loved. In most cases, a man's primary love language is touch and a woman's is gifts. For the woman to want to fulfil the man's primary love language and need, the man must fulfil hers first which will help her want to please him.

This is where a lot of resentment comes in. A woman is expected to please the man with nothing from him in return, apart from maybe a few alcoholic drinks, but isn't it interesting to learn that alcohol is the most commonly used date rape drug.

On some occasions a woman may use alcohol to lose her inhibitions to have fun with a guy, but she is just blocking out any discomfort from the truth.

She is letting a guy use her for his pleasure and may tell herself lies to feel better about it.

To reach the long-lasting relationship with the deepest commitment, you need to feel happy, stable, and secure without a partner first. Therefore, dating many people means you are not relying on only one person, which can make you feel nervous and anxious to be able to feel fully and freely yourself. You will be secure that you have others. You can do this until you find exactly what you want and don't get lost in one man or one woman. You will be encouraged to stay focused on keeping your own self happy and not blaming another for any negative reactions. If you do decide you don't like someone, you will be happy to not string them along.

If you don't like being alone, you may end up dating guys you don't like. If this happens have a break and make a conscious effort to meet up with your friends.

What you must realise when having lots of dates with many different people.

When going on lots of dates with lots of people you will not have the time to establish a true stable connection with one person. Dating lots of people is the first step in making it safe for you to let go and start letting those real feelings come into play when you find the one man or woman committed to you. This strategy makes it possible to develop a stable long-term loving relationship.

A comforting thought for women to know is that usually when a man is fully in love, he is fully in love forever with one woman.

It is usually women who choose to end long term relationships. They got bored; he was too nice. I have been guilty of this in the past, but we deserve nice. We deserve to be loved and cherished.

Women that resonate with this... go out and make excitement for your life in other areas, not with a dangerous man, who is able to screw with your feelings or be a "macho man." What you need to understand with a "macho man" is they have huge egos.

Well, everyone has an ego, even non macho men, but the dangerous ones, they look for a beautiful woman, she makes him look good. It fuels his ego. You, the woman, is the reason he is feeling good about himself. So... why are you selling yourself short? Why are you letting a man make you feel unworthy and not good about yourself? You are the reason he feels good. Find a man that is worthy of you, to make you feel good.

A decent man wants to make you happy. He wants to keep you feeling good. If you feel good, it makes him look good, that he is doing an excellent job of caring for you. That is what love is. Love wants to care and make you feel good, and you naturally want to love in return when you feel it.

You can even create it because it is our natural state. Make a conscious decision to do something loving for someone you don't particularly like and see how good it makes you feel. Don't do something loving in a way that pleases the other so they should give you love and commitment in return, or sex. Do it for yourself. Do it in a way that makes you feel good for you to do without expecting anything in return from the other.

If you keep creating and giving love, but your partner is only ever taking, just get away and leave the situation.

Dating

Only a saint could keep giving love without getting it back. Everyone has an ego and a pain body which gets triggered at times. The person you leave that never gives you love in return, will have to start soul searching and digging deep into themselves. Forcing them to find their soul and true connection to God's love is good for the whole planet.

Sex: Good or Bad?

CHAPTER 10

The Gentle Man

I have met many lovely guys on my journey. They were so sweet and showed me a lot of genuine care. I felt safe with these safe guys, so safe that it felt unsafe to me "What are they after? What is their ulterior motive?" That was my "show love with hate" issue going on.

Feeling safe is where the attraction can start to build. Even though I was scared, I still met with them for practice. Practising feeling safe in the company of a gentle man, I understand the meaning of the word "gentleman" now, GENTLE is the best part of this word.

Do you want love and care or a "macho man"?

Some of these sweet and kind men were very handsome but because they were so laid back and my weird issues of being attracted to a bad guy, I never saw the attractiveness in them. My behaviour towards these kind men was due to childhood trauma, "show love to the men that show me hate", and "show hate to the men that show me love".

Confidence is extremely attractive! Practice makes perfect! Gentleness and confidence combined. Perhaps, the gentlemen I met weren't too confident.

Only when I started to allow myself to feel safe with the *gentle* men, the attractiveness in them, started to appear. If only these shy men could have been less afraid of rejection and were more forward and confident, we both could have gotten to know each other.

A prime example of "what we see in others is a reflection of ourselves".

IF ONLY I HAD BEEN MORE FORWARD AND LESS AFRAID OF REJECTION, OR LESS AFRAID OF BEING LOVED!

I should have known me as the high value woman, could have confidently asked these men I wanted to see them again as a friend. Gentlemen are happy to be in the "friend zone". They are happy to keep their urges under control.

However, I would have expected them to pay, I think that is why I never wanted to ask, because even if a man is put in the "friend zone" something in me wants them to be the guy that I saw in the Disney movies. Which I learnt doesn't happen. I want them to protect and provide. Providing is a form or protection.

I wanted them to make me feel the sexual urge to want to be with them in a relationship. Like I mentioned before, safety is the key. Strong, bold, confidence helps. Toxic men have this, which is why vulnerable women can fall for them.

Many men are afraid of being taken advantage of and used so they're less likely to put their hand in their pocket and offer to pay when they ask you out. However, a woman loves being taken out and it makes us feel looked after and safe.

Safe to get to know them even more. I guess some men are shy because they don't earn a lot and know they can't afford to take a woman out how they would like to. Most women really don't care about money from a man. In my experience it is only a problem when the man wants access to the women's money. When a man wants a woman's money it feels very unsafe and can cause problems.

When a man loves a woman, he loves to provide for her, he wants to protect her and profess (tell the world she is with him). When you understand that a man loves to provide for the woman he loves, you realise the men that take and latch off women, can't know how to love.

It is part of their masculinity to give to her and make her feel safe.

A Very Uncomfortable Date!

When one of the most lifesaving relationship coaches I ever had, coached me to go on every single date with a man that was offered to me, I did.

My pictures and profile on various different internet dating sites attracted loads of messages from guys. Every guy that wanted to meet me, I agreed to it and went on the date. (After a few awful dates I did start to get pickier.)

I started with quick hourly coffee dates, but if lunch or dinner was offered, I would take up that offer too. I was meeting and going on so many dates with guys, I lost count and can't even remember them.

Just like Rori Raye said to do, use them for practice and never pay. Every guy you meet, use them for practice, to speak to and build your confidence, and practice feeling and expressing it.

One day when a new date suggested meeting at 7pm in the evening, I assumed that time meant we would meet for dinner. With my fake confidence, I met him outside on my drive, using Rori's advice.

I smiled a big friendly smile and asked him, "Where are we going?" I was all dressed up and ready for dinner.

His smile was sheepish, and he looked down at the floor. "I don't know this area," he said. His energy was seriously lacking. I already knew I wasn't keen… but decided to carry on and use him for practice.

I realise now I should have felt my authentic feelings and expressed them. "I am looking to feel love and I am not feeling that with you. I don't want to waste your time or mine."

*I also realise, looking back, I had made a big mistake. You should never let a stranger know where you live. You always arrange to meet up in a public place. *

A tip for the men – If you go on a date with a lady and she asks a question for you to make the decision, you need to have a confident answer.

Look up her area on Google maps and have some options she can choose from. A lady wants to be taken care of and feel like the man is stable and strong.

If you expect her to decide where you are taking her on a date, it feels very unsettling, especially as you really need to be the one that pays.

If you don't have a lot of money, a quick coffee isn't anything. You can't expect a lady to decide on the date if you're paying.

If it is the first few dates, the man should definitely expect to pay if he wants to make her feel relaxed and open in his company. It is the gentleman thing to do.

It is not the not the gentleman thing to do if you expect something in return.

Ladies never want to feel like gold diggers, but they do want the man to be able to take care of them, so she can relax and be the feminine woman he desires.

Feeling closed and unsafe isn't attractive for the man or the woman. A desperate man, with an incredibly physically attractive woman by his side, won't care how she is feeling. His ego will feel amazed that he even has her there.

The Gentle Man

A woman that feels good being independent by not needing a man for anything, runs the risk of not being feminine on her dates with men. Being able to lean back, open up and allow him to pay is vulnerable, and allows the man to feel masculine.

In a perfect world it wouldn't matter, but everyone has an ego, especially men as mentioned previously.

Anyway, back to my story...

I decided to be taken to the closest, familiar place I felt comfortable in. He seemed very uncomfortable, and I felt like he didn't want to be there.

We went into the restaurant and when the waiter came to take our order, I was completely horrified. I ordered a delicious paella dish. The waiter asked him for his order, and he said, "No, not for me I am not hungry." I was mortified. I got the message that he didn't want to take me to the restaurant for dinner. Eating alone felt very uncomfortable!

I thought, "Why are we here?" He was awkward and it exposed my painful burning truth; that I was extremely awkward too. I wasn't awkward because I wanted him to like me. I was awkward because I realised how much I didn't want to be there.

He knew nothing about how to make me feel comfortable and at ease. If the money situation was a problem, then he should have gone with my expected plan CONFIDENTLY, or CONFIDENTLY told me he wasn't expecting to take me to dinner.

I have never looked at this before but now it has suddenly dawned on me. Was he expecting to come into my flat into my home on a first date?

Obviously in the past I had made huge mistakes of letting guys into my apartment before realising I was worthy of at least a free coffee in exchange for my time. Since learning to become a high-value woman, I never let a man into my home space without feeling safe and comfortable with them outside my apartment first.

Sex: Good or Bad?

Sometimes a man would bring a bottle of wine with him into my home space, and I would think that it was a lovely, sweet thing to do. I now realise, alcohol is the most used date rape drug.

Men of all statuses will try and invest as little as possible to get into a woman's knickers to feed their ego; but the high value man, would never expect to enter a woman's personal space without getting her to know she is safe with him, without meeting her for a few dates in public first.

I met a guy the other day and he told me he wanted a woman to have a relationship with. I said what you really want is the sex. He agreed that was part of it. There are so many sweet guys that don't get much luck with women.

I asked him... "Who do you need to be in order to get a woman to want to have sex with you?" He wasn't sure. He needs to be confident. He needs to feel powerful and able to protect her, so she can feel safe to open up and be vulnerable. This guy had an incredibly good job and was wealthy.

He has the power to provide and therefore protect. He just didn't have much confidence, especially around women. He had "the chat" as I saw him chatting with a woman, but when I suggested he ask for her number, he was too afraid. I am guessing he was afraid of her saying "no." Guys don't like the word "no" so much, that either they don't accept it, or they refuse to put themselves in a position where they might hear it.

I only came to this realisation after meeting this sweet man the other day. He was obviously the kind of man that would love and adore any woman he got with.

If you're a man that would rather not hear the word "no", then you already are in a position to have a lot more success. You just need to find your power by being able to hear the word "no" and build on it.

Practise hearing the word "no" by allowing yourself to approach a woman and ask her out or ask for her number. Some "bitches" may laugh but inside you will know why you put yourself in that position. To help yourself grow stronger and more confident. Eventually you will not care whether you hear the word "no." Eventually someone will say "yes" - it is the law of averages. When you get the "yes" you can practise not getting your hopes high that she is the one. It may not lead into a relationship but the "yes" will feel so good that it builds up your confidence. But... remember not to get too overly excited. That is the ego placing the responsibility of your good feelings on her.

If you're a shy woman, start out by circular dating, reading this, you can be the one that says "yes" and then practise being vulnerable and open around him when it feels safe to do so and practise and practise some more putting up boundaries! Practice receiving and knowing you're doing good by being kind and building his confidence up but also building up your own confidence.

If the man is not afraid to show his excited and happy feelings, she may find him more attractive to her. It takes confidence to show true feelings. He just needs to make sure it comes from the natural place, and not the place where he makes her the one responsible for the good feelings that arise up in him.

Sex: Good or Bad?

CHAPTER 11

Men Too

I didn't know I was going to have a chapter with this heading when I began my book-writing journey, but I know it is important for many men, especially the men that get triggered by #MeToo.

#MenToo is a social movement in India which was started against false sexual harassment allegations in the #MeToo movement in India. This chapter doesn't talk about false allegations but is about men with #MeToo stories of their own, at the hands of other women.

One day, while on the train home from London, I got chatting to two lads about this book I was still writing at that time. In our conversation, I shared with them a few of my chapter titles, one of them being about #MeToo. As we shared with each other, one of the lads may have been triggered by this and shared what had happened to his friend.

He related how a woman had touched him up without his consent and the trauma he still felt as a result although the incident happened a long time ago. As I listened to this lad's truth, my heart opened to him. I am guessing that he felt triggered by my chapter title #MeToo and wanted to let me know that it happened to men as well.

Instead of feeling triggered by the lad's story, I felt love and compassion as if he were a woman that had been through it, and I could relate. Of course, I could relate, just because his gender was different to mine, it didn't mean he didn't have the same feelings of violation that a woman would have.

I asked him for a consensual hug, and he obliged. He could feel the love and compassion from me. I know he felt safe. I did feel safe with him, even though he was quite clearly drunk. When he thought I felt unsafe, he told me about his wife and showed me a photograph of his baby.

I know this didn't mean he wasn't abusive but with my new-found insights about men, and changing my mindset around men, knowing I attract nice men into my life, I decided I was safe. When I discovered that he had experienced a #MeToo situation, it broke my heart. I am not blaming him, I am just adding that he was drunk, and I remember most of my #MeToo stories, I too had been drunk. Of course, the violating experiences led me onto wanting to drink more alcohol to black it out and numb the pain.

He was not the only man who shared about his sexual abuse from a woman to me. I remember sharing a few jacuzzis with a friend who told me about a similar experience. He was out on holiday, drunk with his friends and he passed out and the woman carried on. He didn't understand why his friends didn't stop her from abusing him. Men do tend to laugh at their friend's trauma instead of taking it seriously. Alcohol will often have a part to play in this. When I ask myself why some men laugh at their friends sexually violating experiences, it makes me wonder why men that make rape jokes find it funny. They then too find it funny if a man is at the expense of it. However, any man that has experienced it knows full well it isn't something to be laughed at.

My Stories as a #MeToo Victim and Perpetrator

During my adolescent years, I had very little self-worth or self-respect. I also had very little understanding of men and didn't think they were interested in relationships, and if they did it certainly wasn't with me. I felt used by men. Taken advantage of. Used for sex only when what I really craved was their love. I felt so disgusted by men's attitudes and lost in the loveless life I was living that I came up with a plan.

I planned to take control of all the sexual experiences. Men want sex, so men can have sex. On one occasion I approached a random man and told him, "Let's go have sex!" He shook his head and replied "No."

I scoffed and said, "What is wrong with you, are you gay or something?" He shook his head again and then stood up and did as I asked. I coerced him into having sex when he had clearly told me "No." At the time I genuinely believed I was innocent of any wrongdoing. He was a man, and that's what men want, is it not?

There was another time when I was drunk in the pub and chatting to a guy. I suggested the same thing to him. After a couple of moments of pondering on his thoughts, he said "yes".

He was very excited on the way back to his grandma's, where he was living. He told me had only been with three other women. I fantasised that we might fall in love or something as he seemed to not be the slutty sort of man or a womaniser.

We had sex in his single bed. Afterwards, he took me back to the Bed and Breakfast where I was staying, in a trolley. I could feel the chilly air against my face, as he pushed the trolley as quickly as he could. He was extremely excited and squealing in delight. On the way back he told me hadn't really been with three women, and that it had only been two women, then he admitted it was only one. I felt weirded out that he had lied to me. I felt violated, like, what was the point of lying to me?

He then admitted the one and only woman he had been with was me. He had been a virgin before meeting me, the seven-teen-year-old girl that had been with many teens and men already. I felt violated and disgusted and couldn't wait to get away from him. He lied. I couldn't stand liars but also what it had been over, why did it matter to lie beforehand?

A few months later, I moved to a YMCA hostel and saw him again. By coincidence, my next-door neighbour was his sister who he had come to visit. "When are we going on that date?" He bellowed. I felt repulsed. He was not the kind of man I was interested in. "YUK! NEVER!" I thought as I blushed at the thought of anyone else around hearing.

Many years later I heard that he had committed suicide. He had had social services involved because there was a rumour going around that he might have been fiddling with his children. Even more years later when I was in college, I met one of his other younger family members. She had deep self-harm scars on her arms, much deeper and thicker in comparison to mine. He had gone and raped her as well.

This is a prime example of toxic behaviour I discuss in the Toxic chapter, creating negative experiences in others like a domino effect.

CHAPTER 12

#MeToo

What is the #MeToo movement?

The #MeToo movement was first created by a courageous woman called Tarana Burke; in 2006. She began to use "#MeToo" to raise awareness of women who had been abused.

The #MeToo movement only became famous in October 2017, when dozens and dozens of sexual abuse allegations came out against Harvey Weinstein. Alyssa Milano was the courageous actress who first came out about him on Twitter, and her tweet ended up going viral.

How does it make you feel?

Whether you have only just learnt about #MeToo or you have known about it for a long time, whether you are a man or a woman; how does it make you feel?

The first step to healing is being aware of how you really feel about it and sit with it. Whether you're a man or a woman, how you feel is totally valid and normal.

As a woman with my own #MeToo stories, I can tell you that at first, I was shocked. Shocked at how many women there actually were with horror stories at the hands of an abusive man. Really shocked!

Then I was amazed. Amazed because, yes, #MeToo. I felt

relieved. I was not the only one.

I thought if us women speak out together, will this finally end? Will we finally be loved? I felt I had to hold onto my story, it then made my ego feel powerful instead of weak and silent. #MeToo meant that I had to stay strong, and no man could ever hurt me again.

Then I started to feel fear. I was afraid because of the number of women speaking out and the growing numbers of women, meant growing numbers of abusive men. (I realise now that the men that abuse women, abuse more than one, so the number of women being abused isn't equal to the number of men abusing which is a relief to know about.)

Not only did it put fear in me because of the growing numbers, but I saw so many men were reacting negatively to it on social media and were starting to show hatred towards women. That is what my consciousness witnessed. Misogynistic comments started to grow too. I felt horrified.

At first, my defence mechanism shot up! "How dare you!" To the obviously uncaring, guilty man. Or "How could you?" To men I saw as kind and caring, and men I saw as the good guys. "Do you not understand the pain and torment I and other women have been through? Do you not realise how difficult it is to speak up about it? How long have we kept silent about it? How dare you! You MUST be guilty!"

It left a bad taste in my mouth, and I started to resent the good guys. I felt victimised even more and deeply hurt. The rage I had managed to control as a teenager, started to bubble up.

I had severe anger issues as an adolescent. If a man gave me bad feelings I would rage, blame and hate them and want to get my revenge on them.

I managed to control my anger, by finding a connection and praying to what some call God. Anger is healthy to be able to communicate, if as long as you don't blame your partner and assume they made you angry on purpose and you share how you feel rather than express it in an angry rage.

Usually, underneath the anger is a different feeling you felt unable to express. Something uncomfortable that feels disempowering, too overly vulnerable. I realised deep down I had developed a hatred towards men. I realised that "How is this going to help me get what I really desperately want?" What was this hatred?

It was fear.

Fear of #MeToo

Once I realised men weren't going to stop abusing women just because of #MeToo and I realised that good men didn't like feeling responsible for all the bad men in the world; whenever I saw #MeToo anywhere on social media, I felt triggered and in a timid helpless dark hole.

Once I was aware of the fear I felt around #MeToo, I had to consciously make myself unafraid. Whenever I saw or heard something that had nothing to do with abuse and my response was "me too;" the fear I felt made me change my words to something like "I had that experience." I had to change the words, so I didn't feel fear.

The fear got quite bad, and I realised I needed to face this fear head on. I didn't want to live in fear anymore.

Whenever I could reply to something with the words "me too." I made sure I did use them. I felt the fear associated with it, but I stayed aware and dissolved it. I do the same now, but I don't feel any fear seeing the words #MeToo at all. It doesn't trigger me at all.

I guess men, feel triggered by #MeToo, because it threatens the connection they crave to make with a woman.

Sex: Good or Bad?

How I got to this conclusion

What I wanted more than anything was a happy and successful, fulfilling relationship. I wanted to be loved and adored. A lot of the relationships that didn't work out because I was just being used, added towards my disgust about men and viewing them as a species that only want sex.

I had to stop and put my pain aside, I had to let it frazzle. I had to make myself see it from their point of view. I made a lot of discoveries. I even found love and compassion for the nastiest abuser. I saw all men being made to feel responsible even if they hadn't done anything wrong to a woman ever.

Some men can't handle that responsibility. They see it as an attack. They see it as being blamed. When we come from a place of pure love, and lifting the planets' frequency, we don't want others to feel bad. We want everyone to feel loved and accepted.

So, as a woman I had to do my best to heal my hurt so I could make men feel loved and not responsible or blamed.

It hurt more, when the negative response around #MeToo came from men who were my friends and I saw them as good men. Not highly sexy and sought after men, but men I saw as friends and thought they would have my back and see me as being brave and have them stick by me.

These men had never done anything to me. At some points in my life, they were all I really felt I had, and I needed them. I am not a woman with loads of female friends that I see and talk to regularly.

I had to stop and let the pain I felt frazzle. I had to feel the pain and surrender my own ego. I made myself see it from their point of view. I made a lot of discoveries. I even found love and compassion for the nastiest abuser. It got me into an extremely dangerous situation but being able to feel fully authentic and feel ALL my feelings I was luckily saved by a male onlooker. I will talk about that more a bit later. (I realise now it was also my show hate with love issue.)

Even the good men feel attacked. They feel that women hate all men. It isn't that at all, but it made me wonder why they thought this.

If you're a man and you feel these things... Do you have an answer for me?

Dig deep into the truth however uncomfortable it may feel and don't be afraid to share it. The world needs everyone's authentic truth.

Women want to be heard and listened to because we feel afraid in this world. There was an incident that occurred that I learnt from Teal Swan's YouTube channel, where there was a room full of men and women.

A question was asked to all the men, "How many men have feared for their life at some point?" Not many of the hands went up. The same question was asked to the women and every single one of the women's hands went up.

When you learn about trauma and its effect on the brain and people, you realise that it is always there forever. Unless you discover Adam Mussa's work, you can dissipate it and dissolve it completely. I am so grateful to have discovered Adam Mussa along with many other great teachers and healers in the world, Eckhart Tolle author of "The Power of Now".

Living a happy and fulfilled life isn't easy with unresolved trauma. A person with PTSD or CPTSD, can be triggered by anything minor that can send them into a flashback where they feel just as afraid as they did when the trauma occurred.

Fearing for your life is a traumatic feeling. Some of these women may have experienced it on a minor level but others may have experienced it first hand, fully.

Suffering from PTSD, anything can trigger those feelings of horror. When you look back in history and how it was ok to cane your wife, "the rule of thumb" saying comes from when men were allowed to cane their wives if they didn't like something she did. The cane was not allowed to be any thicker than their thumb. Quite a horrifying fact to learn.

That is trauma and trauma stays in the genes and is passed on through generations if it is unresolved. It may be passed on in other ways and mutate into something different but it is still there.

If you go even further back in history where witch hunts took place and women were executed in horrific ways, all of that is traumatic and has been passed down through generations. Women fear a lot more than men do, and they're in fear because of men.

Catcalling

Casually walking along the street, minding my own business, and getting on with my day, I have walked past a group of males so many times, either walking past them in the street or them being at work, (usually trades workmen) (I guess you don't usually walk past men working in offices) and I have been whistled at or been "complimented" on the way I look.

It would shake me up and I would suddenly be made to feel nervous. A stranger suddenly interrupted my day. My Dad always warned me of strangers as a kid, so there was a bit of learnt fear from there.

I was often bullied at school for being "fat" and sometimes "ugly." So, I didn't have very good self-esteem.

When I was younger and I first started experiencing compliments and wolf whistles, the nervous feeling I felt was flattering and a bit exciting. I couldn't believe I was thought to be attractive! It felt like positive attention to me, and I would flash a shy smile, blushing. This would often give the male onlooker the wrong opinion. It would wrongly make him think it was ok to approach me and ask for my number and I would always feel like I had to oblige, out of fear. Fear of upsetting him and making him feel rejected.

My mother always taught me it was important to be polite. So, I never wanted to reject anyone and feel like I was being rude. This behaviour of mine would have taught him that catcalling a woman in the streets was acceptable.

It taught me that looking beautiful and sexy was a way to capture a man's attention. I thought it was a way to keep a man attached to you emotionally too, but that is not the case.

It never dawned on me that the type of man that does catcall women in the streets, is a low value type of man. Enjoying cheap attention is also low value. I had to learn the hard way. Men are visual and most men may look at a gorgeous looking, sexy woman but most men don't express themselves verbally or forcefully.

When you understand how our brains are wired to survive, they're wired to remember the negative circumstances in order to avoid the negative cycle repeating itself. So, when you are constantly catcalled or harassed in the street, these negative connotations stand out and give all other men a bad name.

As I got older, I soon learned to find the men that catcalled me in the street very offensive. I realised the shaking up nervous feeling I felt was fear and the fear was there for a good reason.

Since the #MeToo movement began. I once walked past a couple of men at work and one of them yelled something at me. (I am now so zoned out from what is happening around me, a type of survival, that I don't notice these things.)

The reason I suddenly remembered this occasion was that the other man butted in and said something to him and then gave me an apologetic look. I suddenly felt aware of what had happened and I felt safe. I also felt a sudden attraction to the man caring for the alone woman walking in the street, me.

It's just a joke

I have at times heard some very triggering "jokes" that the

man delivering thinks is funny. It is not funny. Here are some examples:

- Commenting on someone's body parts.

- Any form of rape or sexual assault joke

- Any joke where they pretend to touch you up

- Violent jokes

- Blonde jokes

- Housework and kitchen jokes

You get the gist of things, there are many more examples. As a woman that has survived horrific crimes, it jolts me and forces me into freeze mode. It feels extremely uncomfortable. The dumb blonde jokes and the housework and kitchen jokes are just boring, but the subconscious mind takes it in and makes me feel like I am not able or worthy of doing anything else. I am guessing some men's ego wants this and enjoys it even if they are unaware of what they are doing.

I have witnessed women as well as men laughing at the jokes, making the joke seem acceptable and it goes into the subconscious minds of everyone listening, so that if either of them finds themselves in a serious situation, at the back of some men's minds they think it is just a joke and can get away with it, or women will find it hard to report because they think they're being silly to cause a fuss because it is "just a joke".

If you're ever a bystander, sticking up for women and calling out the person that makes a joke can make you look super powerful, secure in yourself and genuinely kind and caring. You may be rejected from the group but realise that you have made a significant impact on sharing the truth and the truth always prevails. The higher power of the truest love will put you on a good path of rewards.

Once I was out in public somewhere and I overheard two couple's conversations. One made a sexist comment, it was very minor and mild, that I even managed to find a smile in me for it, THIS IS A SMILE FROM A WOMAN, we are so used to hearing sexist remarks, it is drummed into many women to find it funny too, and told it is funny, even when it is not funny and just a stupid thing to say. I found it funny because I have a deeper understanding of men and also why women act how they may sometimes act. Women are in pain. If I was stuck in my ego, I would have found it offensive instantly.

The guy from the other couple, not forcefully, not completely timidly but a little bit, I guess he felt nervous, or perhaps he was just being a GENTLE man, he said something along the lines of "that is sexist."

I melted and thought how wonderful he was and how lucky his wife was to have such a caring gentleman by her side.

If you are in a group and manage to call out sexism, behind the "joker's" back you will find that other members of the group congratulate you for not being afraid, but afraid at the time to share their true thoughts in front of the "joker."

What sort of energy do you want to be around, the kind of people with energy that keeps you in low vibes, or sort out truth seekers and be around powerful people so you too can learn to be powerful?

Sex: Good or Bad?

CHAPTER 13

Trust

The most important part of any relationship is trust. You must be able to trust your partner, the person you're committed to, and feel an attachment with.

If you're a person with a history of heartbreak, pain and in some cases trauma, then you may find it very difficult to completely trust. So, how do you learn to trust? Before you can trust another person, you must first learn to trust yourself. If you've had a heart break in the past, it is easy to either blame yourself or your ex-partner.

No one is to blame fully apart from the ego. Both parties have an ego and ego's love to aggravate the other's ego. If your ex-partner betrayed you, then they must have had a need they wanted fulfilled that unfortunately you were unable to do or felt comfortable allowing them to do or they were not able to communicate for whatever reason, or they were completely unaware.

Either you will blame them for betraying you or blame yourself for not fulfilling their needs. The ego loves to blame causing pain.

What comes with trust is communication. For a happy and healthy relationship, communication is vitally important and to be able to fully communicate with your partner, you must be able to trust them, to be able to be fully yourself with them.

If you can't communicate with your partner, then there will be no trust. So how do you trust them, to be able to communicate?

Sex: Good or Bad?

The first thing you must do is to be able to trust yourself. You practise putting boundaries in place and trusting yourself that you will keep your boundaries in place. If someone calls you or texts you late at night, when you would normally be sleeping, you must trust yourself to look after yourself and care for your own needs, which is to get a suitable amount of rest and sleep each night.

You tell the late-night caller that you don't take phone calls past a certain time, 9pm or a time that suits you and you must stick to it. When you do this, don't get caught up in the late-night conversations that can go on for hours into the night and you feel like you're getting lost in the other person. You stick to your guns and stay in control of yourself and set good boundaries for yourself. You remind yourself who is the boss. You are!

Doing this shows the other that you are high value, and you value your time, and you prioritise yourself over them.

That is one tip to make yourself attractive. You're not doing it to be attractive though, you're doing it to show yourself you're in control of yourself and have boundaries that you're entitled to have, and to test him to see if he tries to push down your barriers.

However, you may be ok with late night calls and still feel in control of yourself. There will be other things you can put in place to set a boundary. Every time you prioritise yourself over another and stick to your boundary, you are showing everyone and yourself that you prioritise yourself over letting someone break down your boundary.

You can be strict with this too. You will learn if another person respects you enough to listen to you and not try to break down your boundary. If they don't respect you, you know that they will end up not respecting you in other areas.

Another boundary you may set in place for yourself is no one coming into your apartment until you feel comfortable and have established a certain level of relationship or friendship with them that you are happy to let them into your home.

Trust

Setting boundaries also creates an element of mystery about you, which is super highly attractive and gets whoever you have your eye on thinking about you.

Another thing you can do to learn to trust yourself and your partner, is to practise the feeling messages I discussed in the "Feelings" chapter. It will be scary, but you need to feel the fear and let it dissolve.

If you don't trust your partner and you can't communicate very well with your partner, the sex isn't going to be very fulfilling. When you can fully trust yourself and your partner and you can effectively communicate, the sex, the chemistry and love and connection will be incredible. It will be out of this world.

First, trust yourself, so you know that you're safe. I talk more about safety in the"Feelings" chapter.

Also, when you can fully trust your partner and feel completely safe with them, you are free to experiment any way you wish to, without the worry of what they will think.

However, if you do this under the influence of alcohol, you're not actually connecting emotionally. You're blocking yourself of from being able to connect from the true source of love, deep within that connects to your creator.

Feel free and have fun!

Sex: Good or Bad?

CHAPTER 14

Communicate

I t is so important that men and women both communicate exactly what they want with each other. Either they will want the same as you or you will both know it is time to move on.

Always, practise the tips I speak about in the "feelings" chapter but as well as that you need to be bold and strong and say exactly what it is you want from the other.

Feeling protected and having your boundary up is a good feeling to have and to practise having.

When I was in my mid-twenties there was one man that I really liked a lot and felt it was love. When we started hooking up, he showed me signs of really liking me too. But at the time I believed that any man I had sex with was only interested in me for that. I was mortified if I ever caught on to any feelings and there was no way I could allow myself to show them.

I had my son at this stage, and I wasn't comfortable having another man in my son's life and I didn't believe that he would want to be with a single mother anyway.

I believed single mothers get used quite a lot. They're easier because they are busy with their child. He took me fishing; he bought my son chocolate gifts. I never had that from any man before. I felt afraid and wondered why he was doing that. I realise now it was because he was a nice man, and he did actually like me. I didn't believe it though. I was set in my ways of my old beliefs. "Men only want me for sex!"

I always had a belief that because I lived in a council property, I wasn't worthy of love. I wasn't good enough to be with, or any man that did show me love there was something wrong with him or there was a hidden agenda.

I didn't think I was tidy enough or clean enough either. I really liked him, but I became quiet and shy around him. I enjoyed the time we spent together, and I liked seeing him, but I always thought he just wanted me for sex because I was giving it to him. That was my belief.

Because of my belief I felt pain. I desperately wanted to be in a proper relationship with him, but I felt unable to communicate. I also thought there was no point. If he wanted me for love and a relationship, then he would say something to me. I didn't know it was up to me as the woman to make a relationship happen. If he was just using me for sex, then it was up to me to say something and find out what his motive was with me. Then I would be able to get rid of him swiftly. Men don't know what they want. They just know they like being around a woman and getting whatever she gives him.

I always felt timid and shy after having sex with a man I liked and wanted a deeper connection with. I was scared if I did say something and my worries were true, then I wouldn't get to see him again. That is how low my self-esteem was. I should have not cared and communicated EXACTLY what I wanted! If I didn't get it, then I should have been the one ditching him!

(My beliefs have changed now too. I know that there are many lonely men that feel disconnected out there, that would love to experience a true connection with a woman. I also know that there are many men out there that help with the housework too if you struggle.)

I guess I was timid and shy because I was partly ashamed because of past traumas coming up, and memories of the past. I just assumed he didn't care about me and would naturally be like the others. If he wanted a relationship with me, he would have told me.

Because of my belief, the way I stopped obsessing and pining over a man I would meet other guys. So, I attempted to do this when it was offered. Looking back, it may have been a trap to see if I was genuine or not.

The guy I liked more than anything stopped seeing me. I was heartbroken even more. I should have felt what I felt and communicated it. I did not feel in the position to do so. The problem was if he really wanted me then why didn't he tell me? That is what I thought.

I thought "if a man can have sex with me, then a man can talk to me".

That is another example of "what we see in others is a reflection of ourselves," We were both not communicating when we both should have been communicating. He was a reflection of me, and my own behaviour and I was projecting it onto him and what he should have been doing.

It is thoroughly important to communicate before you have sex with someone so you both know you're on the same page as each other.

A lot of times in my life it has just been a guessing game, confusion, and pain. Mostly being used and abused and letting them get away with it. Not having any boundaries and hoping one day one of these men would be the hero I craved.

I remember a guy I was sleeping with sometime before I met my husband and married him. I really believed the guy wasn't interested in me for anything more and I felt too embarrassed and ashamed to communicate my feelings.

I met him on a specific dating site which made me believe he wouldn't want me for anything more than a quick fling.

I didn't believe I was worthy of anything more, which is why I found myself dabbling on those websites in the first place. I used all the tools I knew about, and it did work. I just didn't know and was oblivious to it. I didn't have the extra information of just coming out with it bluntly and saying it in black and white.

It was only after I got married that he expressed his true feelings to me verbally. I am committed to God, and I love my husband dearly, so nothing would have been able to happen anyway.

The greatest thing about my husband is I feel safe with him to communicate anything to him however awful and horrible I may feel about what I am saying. He always does what he can to make me feel better and I am aware of this, and I do all the inner work to feel grateful for him in every moment. Gratitude is the greatest thing we can feel for our partners so that we can have the best loving relationship. The more gratitude you feel, the more love you can feel.

More examples to get what you want from a man

When I was 24, I went out with a friend shopping for an outfit to wear on a night out. I had been working out at the gym and had a lovely slim curvy size 12 figure. I found a stunning black and white mini dress that hugged my curves nicely. It was short and showed off my toned legs.

I curled my blonde hair, did my make-up to enhance my already pretty face and teamed it with a pair of black heels.

With all the compliments my friends gave me about how amazing I looked I felt like a million dollars.

On my drunken walk home, I ended up taking off my shoes to walk in bare foot. I saw a couple of lads walking past and I jokingly and drunkenly asked if I could wear his shoes.

His initial reaction was "No, no you cannot!" I wasn't offended as it was partly a joke and an excuse to have some company.

After he caught a glimpse of me, he changed his tune quickly.

"Ok, yes sure. Yes, you can!"

I was happy to have my feet protected in shoes that weren't painful to walk in.

A bit further up we spotted my friend in a kebab shop. After some friendly interaction he ended up putting her in a taxi and paying for it for her to get home.

I suddenly felt paranoid about his actions. I took off his shoes and said "bye" and ran off up the hill leaving him and his shoes.

I didn't get very far, and he was running up the hill after me. "Where are you going? Where are my shoes?" He seemed a bit annoyed.

"I left them down there" I pointed. He went back down the hill after his shoes. I was relieved as I had gotten rid of him.

I wasn't expecting him to come back up the hill and find me, but he did.

"These are very expensive shoes!" He still sounded annoyed.

"I'm sorry," I said genuinely. I could tell he was a nice man, but I didn't find nice men attractive. "Please can I wear your shoes again?"

He took off his shoes again and let me wear them.

We got into a conversation, and I told him I really loved going to Turkey on holiday and I didn't have quite enough saved up to go back.

"How much do you need?"

"200 pounds" I replied.

"I'll give it to you!" He said.

"No, no no! I can't accept that." Isn't it so funny how when a large sum of money is offered most people's instant reaction is they can't accept it. Like they're not worthy of it?

Sex: Good or Bad?

It went silent for a little time as I got thinking after the initial shock of such a grand gesture.

My desperation to get back to Turkey was stronger than my need to be polite. I thought it would be OK if I paid him back.

"Ok. I will pay you back though!"

I think he suddenly realised what he had said. "Oh, there are no cash machines around here anyway."

"Yes, there is... there is one right over there!" I pointed a few yards behind us and across the road.

I walked to the cash machine, and he followed me. He put his card in the wall and attempted to withdraw the money. The machine declined his card.

"Oh, it is not working. I have taken out the maximum limit already."

I was sick of men saying things and not sticking to their word. I was sick of men using me and not giving me anything in return and I really did not care about the presence of this man. I cared more about the pain of being let down AGAIN!

"See! I knew you were lying!" I snapped in disgust.

"Ok, Ok, Ok!" He said!! He then took out £100 from the machine and opened up his wallet and took out another £100 and gave it to me.

I looked at it in amazement. "WOW!" I squealed in excitement. I felt like I had won the lottery.

I turned to him, "Thank you! Thank you! Thank you! I will pay you back, I promise!"

"No, don't worry about it!" I knew in my heart I would pay him back. That was my intention. I felt bad taking such a large sum of money from him. It wasn't really that much money but to me it was a lot at that time.

He continued to walk me home and I continued to be amazed and thanked him some more.

We got to my front door and it was time to say "good night" and go our separate ways. I suddenly felt so guilty turning him away. I had let men I didn't like or want to be with in my home and they had never given me anything.

I decided to let him in and sleep on the sofa. It was a silly and dangerous idea but I had survived before and at least he had given me some money.

I knew he was a good young man as I hadn't been initially attracted to him.

Even so I slept with the money under my pillow in fear he would take it back. Bizarre!

In the morning as he was about to leave, I gave him my number. I also felt bad again and asked him if he wanted the money back. He declined and said it didn't matter.

We both felt obliged to meet up again and we did. He took me for an amazing dinner on our first date. We went to the cinema and a few other dates. We did end up sleeping together. I partly felt like I had to because of the money and dates we went on. After that the feelings kicked in and I really wanted a relationship with him. This was before I learnt the all the tools and learnt about men.

I gave him a card with £100 in and said I would pay him the other £100 soon. He wouldn't accept the money back.

He was a true gentleman. A real sweetheart! A blessing on my journey!

Another time on a night out, my male friends' friend took a liking to me. At the end of the night, I realised someone had stolen my coat. He told me that he would buy me a new one.

Again, I wasn't too fussed on him, I was just fussed about not being lied to by a man again and taken for a ride. I wasn't going to be a push over! I kept on about the new coat he said he would buy me to make sure he knew I wasn't going to let it slide and let him get away with not buying me a new coat.

Because I let my male friend stay over, I let him stay over too and I ended up sleeping with him. I was done with being shy and timid around guys I slept with and in the morning, I reminded him again about the coat. I think I also felt safe because I had my male friend there.

Later, the same day, my buzzer went, and it was the guy from the night before with my new coat. It was lovely! I loved that coat! I saw him again after that but then the feelings kicked in and wanting a relationship. I never knew how to get it so I was always left feeling pain and wishing the guy would call or message me.

However, these two stories show that as long as you're bold and up front asking for something, a good man will give it and stick to it. If you act like you don't really care, the man won't really care either and won't see it as a priority.

If you're in a relationship, finding you're vulnerable feeling messages will help, alongside giving compliments for being good at the task. It is much harder to get what you want from anyone by blaming them for your negative feelings or making someone feel bad.

CHAPTER 15

Money

"Gold digger" is a negative term used to describe a woman that only wants a man for his money. I used to be terrified of being seen as a "gold digger." I only wanted a man to love and be loved in return. I felt that wanting a man to buy me gifts and spend money on me wasn't being loving and I would scare the man away as he would see me as a "gold digger".

If I yearned for a man's love, I felt I had to spend my money on him and buy him gifts to show him I wasn't a gold digger and I was in-fact a good woman to be with.

It was a way to express my love to him as well. It is my primary love language. My old belief caused me a lot of suffering with men, and it stemmed from witnessing my parents' divorce when I was about 8 years old. It was extremely heart-breaking having to leave my father, being torn away from him.

My father tried to get custody of all 4 of his children and there was a distressing court battle. I don't remember my mother saying too many horrible things about my dad to me, but I did hear her one evening on the phone to my dad, and she called him a "fucking bastard".

It hurt me a lot to hear her talk to him like that, my special dad, the apple of my eye. There was a time when we all still lived under the same roof and my mum and dad were arguing, my dad accidentally let slip, "darling." A nice loving word.

Sex: Good or Bad?

"Don't call me darling!" Mum snapped back at him in a rage. "I'm sorry, it just slipped out." He replied. It pained me and stung me at a deep level. I adored my dad to pieces. He was the most wonderful man. He was my entire world and I idolised him.

Unfortunately, when my parents divorced, my father did use harsh words about my mother. He said she only wanted him for his money.

When he started having financial problems, that is when she wanted to divorce him. My Dad loved my mum to bits, and he loved all his children to bits, so he was very hurt, and his experience was that she was a "gold digger."

He could no longer provide for her, everything she was used to having before his financial difficulties. He was stressed because of his circumstances and then my mum being angry with him about it, would add to his stress.

One day, I was eating a packet of walker's salt and vinegar crisps. The adverts on TV showed there was money hidden in some of the packets of crisps, inside a little blue envelope. I crunched down on a crisp or two, then when I peered inside the crisp packet, at the silver foil, I noticed a reflection of blue on the side.

"OMG! Is it?" I stopped in awe.

It was! It was blue! I rummaged through the packet and there it was, the little blue envelope! I screamed in delight, "I won. I won. I won!" ignoring the rest of the crisps I ran around the glass coffee table before deciding to go and find my dad. I could end all his financial troubles.

I found my dad with my mum in the hallway upstairs arguing. I was so excited. I knew my dad played the lottery and I had just won this for us.

My mum took the blue envelope from me and opened it. It was a voucher for another packet of crisps. Not as exciting as I thought!

What my mum then said was... "oh, for a moment there, I

thought WE..." (Looking at me and her and then giving my dad a dirty look to say, "not you.") "I thought WE had won lots of money!" My heart sank. I wanted my dad to have it. It hurt my feelings a lot. I loved my dad so much because he really made me feel loved and adored and I wanted to show him all the love in return. I knew money would relieve his stress.

It was painful being separated from my dad, but it was just as painful knowing my dad was in pain not having his children around him. I could also sense his loss of power due to having less money, but it didn't change the love I had for him.

Money or no money, my dad always felt powerful to me. I loved Dad so much and idolised him that whatever he said I believed to be true. He often said harsh things about my mum to me. It made me hate my mum for treating my dad so badly and I blamed her for the separation pain I felt, no longer being able to live with my dad.

Many years later, however; my dad said to me that poisoning young kids' minds against the other parent should be illegal, against the law. (It is now, I believe.) I don't know whether he was admitting to what he did was wrong or had some other reason for saying it but remembering everything he used to say about mum did come to my mind. I struggled with connecting and bonding with my mum and anything she did that I saw as being wrong, was highlighted to me brightly. Evidence that what my dad said about her was right.

I never wanted to be a gold digger. It was confusing though because my dad was always striving to make his money back, so I saw that money was important to a man to feel powerful and women like powerful alpha-type men.

When I was attracted to a powerful alpha man that had plenty of money, I felt a huge wave of guilt in me, and I was unable to feel my true authentic feelings about him.

It isn't the money that is attractive, but the power the man

Sex: Good or Bad?

feels behind having the money and being able to show his love by providing and protecting and in turn making a woman feel safe and secure.

I learnt from reading "The five love languages" by Gary Chapman, that my primary love language is receiving gifts, so for a man to be able to make me feel loved he was always going to have enough money to be able to spoil me, as well as survive with the basics; but only once I conquered my love/hate polarity issue. (Thank you Adam Mussa).

My guilt from finding wealthy men attractive stopped me from getting with a wealthy man. I thought I had to be a "good" girl and show my love to men without receiving anything from them.

When I was old enough to go to pubs and bars, I felt excited being bought alcoholic drinks by a man, like I had achieved something great. I thought if he wanted my time, then he wanted a relationship with me, but I also felt guilty and like I owed him something in return.

I would end up becoming intimate with him easily. I never felt good afterwards and I always hoped he would call to meet up again and give me the relationship I wanted, and knew I was worthy of and deserving, like all women are. I have since learnt that alcohol is the most used date rape drug and also, if a guy wants to buy me a drink to have a conversation with me then he does so just to have a conversation with me and I owe him nothing in return; just enjoy the conversation. This day and age you have to be severely careful that no one spikes your drink with drugs.

I wasn't happy but I was determined I wasn't ever going to be the gold digger type. It was hard because I heard about the amount of money high-class escorts earnt and I knew I had the good looks to be able to do that, but I had my morals, and I couldn't bear the social stigma attached to that. I thought one day, one of these guys will turn around and love me and give me a happy ever after relationship.

I eventually got the message that men didn't like easy women; they get called "slags". Many men will sleep with a "slag", but he doesn't feel good because it was easy. He didn't get to use his instinctive hunting intuition that is built in his genes.

I managed to have a different mindset around it. So, when I did end up again in bed with a guy, I would hope he would be the one. The pain would come back. Sometimes, I would see a guy for a few months thinking that it was a relationship or one day it would be a relationship, but it never came to fruition.

To somehow deal with the pain I thought it would be a clever idea to start acting like a man. Have sex and don't care about it. Sometimes two-timing guys. What did it matter? I didn't care. I had to tell myself I didn't care but deep-down underneath, I really cared. All men wanted was sex. That is how it looked to me.

Even so, I still didn't want to be a gold digger. I didn't want to be an escort even though they earned so much money and I knew I could earn a lot too, but I had my morals, and I was desperate not to go against my morals.

I was Godly and because of God, I wanted to stay on that path. It felt like a lonely path, but I always witnessed incredible things by staying true to God.

I am sure some women that do that job do feel empowered financially where they feel like they work for themselves, however, they are still relying on men for their survival and income.

I am sure some women are desperate for money and don't see any other way and when they try it, it seems easy. Just block off your feelings. Think good feelings about money. But, what about love? God? The truth? Connection? We must never cut off from our feelings. Women that do these jobs usually end up in severely toxic and unhealthy relationships.

I remember a speaker that I can imagine has ended up in a lot of strip clubs and spoken to many women, he said "strippers in strip clubs have great jobs, but they usually end up in violent relationships."

Sex: Good or Bad?

You can imagine these women being the kind of woman that says, "I don't need a man!" When in-fact they're entertaining mostly men for all their income and survival needs. As a woman myself I know what women really need and want, it is to feel safe, loved, and cared for, money does that and many women's primary love language is gifts.

I saw a post on Facebook recently that said, "If she has her own job, her own car, pays her bills and lives comfortably, understand that she wants loyalty, not your money. She can finance herself!"

I view posts like these as a very subtle "give me attention, I am the good kind of woman". That is my opinion. I also used to post memes like that, and that was my deep underlying reason for posting. Then I learnt about men and thought "f**k it!" Life is hard enough! I want love and connection; like most people in this day and age crave.

I commented the following on the Facebook post,

"Get a man to invest in you... With his time and attention, but also with his money and he will be 100% loyal to you.

I used to be afraid to be seen as a gold digger...but then I learnt about men... I don't give a F**k anymore.

You know when a man loves you because of the 3 P's...

He will PROFESS – be proud to tell the world about you.

He will PROTECT – do everything to keep you protected and looked after.

He will PROVIDE – spend money on you and enjoy it. He won't want you to spend your money.

A problem we have these days is people not appreciating each other because of past mishaps and fears of it happening again and being super cautious.

I learnt the 3 P's in a book by Steve Harvey called, "Act like a lady, Think like a Man." (A man that had the nick name "Thomas Crown" recommended it to me. I later realised where the name came from. A character in a film was a rich playboy. He offered to buy me something sparkly but I politely declined even though my insides screamed "yes". I wished he didn't ask and just did it. He obviously thought I needed the book.)

It was the first book I ever purchased and read on relationships and men."

I was politely disagreed with and I totally understood the reply I was given as that used to be my own frame of mind.

I replied...

"Spot on... but I was never successful like that and was often heart broken. I HAD to learn about men and myself.

I definitely agree with being independent and being able to look after yourself... it is a fabulous freeing feeling not having to depend on anyone. It is also safe.

However, if a man you like wants to offer to pay for something for you... if you like spending time with him...

Surrendering your ego and letting him pay will keep him around. Even if it is terrifying! Because it can be terrifying! He needs to feel masculine.

Allowing him to give you love (paying for something is a sign of love) it shows him you are feminine and able to receive him (absolutely terrifying though).

There are men out there that just want to take and take and take, and this can be a test to see if he is a good capable of loving man or a taker. Selfish in it for himself man.

Us women need to look after ourselves. (We're forced to; which is where the happy to be independent comes in.)

It is also important, to feel safe to let in a good man that does want to love and knows how to love.

Sex: Good or Bad?

People that have experienced abuse in childhood find it very difficult... when someone shows love, they have to add hate into the equation... yet when they're shown hate they can't help but show love back to them.

The same cycle often repeats itself, because the abused are used to it... it is familiar to them.

Love is scary because they're not familiar to it... they think there is some nasty hidden agenda to why they're being shown love.

Yep...it is a pretty deep topic! Lol!"

I didn't get a reply, I didn't need one. I just needed to share my heart.

If you as a man feel resentment for making a woman, feel loved and buying her gifts, then maybe your primary love language isn't being fulfilled. When you are in a loving relationship, you want the other to feel loved and you want to feel love. You both need to make an effort to fulfil each other's primary love language.

Either that or you had a past experience where that happened and you're reluctant to go there again.

I know that feeling! I am sending you love!

I learnt from Rori Raye that receiving is a feminine trait and giving is a masculine trait. So, when I was giving gifts to men, I was not being in my feminine and of course I would have been turning them off and not getting them to fall in love with me. However, you can give if it isn't painful or makes you feel resentful. We should always give from our heart so it feels good and not give to expect a reward in return. The reward is in the giving. I used give to show the man I liked him and to show I was good to be with. It felt good but underneath I had a fear of him not giving me the relationship I wanted, and that would make me feel resentful.

Steve Harvey's book "Act like a lady, think like a man" taught me that you will know when a man is in love with you because he wants to provide as well as profess and protect. I found it fascinating and knew I needed to learn to start receiving.

Learning about men, you realise that they fall in love by investing in you, that includes their money as well as their time. They also feel manly by fixing things for you. You can watch a man and see if he does these things.

I learnt from an intelligent guy selling a course to trauma survivors, Adam Mussa, that trauma survivors have many different opposing polarities and one of them is, when someone shows them love, they match it with hate, or when someone shows them hate they show them love, as that is what they're used to as an abuse survivor growing up.

Going back to a lot of the good men I dated, I think I believed there must be something wrong with them if they liked or loved me, paid for dinners and drinks and took me out to nice places. I wondered if there was something wrong with them, or if they had a hidden agenda. I could never properly relax.

This was an amazing and good realisation I had, and it really helped me learn to start accepting the love I was given.

Knowing that accepting is a feminine trait and giving is a masculine trait, it makes sense when looking at the physical act of love and connecting, sex.

The man gives his lingam, which translates as a "wand of light", or to put it more bluntly penis to the woman and she receives it in her yoni, or to put it more bluntly vagina.

"Wand of light" is a beautiful description for a man's' penis. Especially for a woman with a lot of traumatic experiences from men making them often have a negative and shameful reaction and feelings.

If you need to start healing, you can begin to think of a man's penis as a wand of light.

Knowing that giving is more of a masculine trait, when we as women want to give and give and do wonderful things for a man, it is being more masculine, doing, instead of being.

We can do things while being in a being state, but if we do them in order, please a man and hope for a commitment it won't ever work. Remember he is a hunter; he needs to do things to win the woman over.

If you're a woman and you find yourself a man that does things for you and takes you out, never forget to express gratitude.

If you're a man in a relationship, make sure you always express gratitude for your woman too.

Notice everything your partner does that you can feel gratitude for. When someone feels appreciated, they want to do more for you. As someone that has SURVIVED trauma, it can feel uncomfortable when someone does something kind for you, you can sometimes feel afraid. Learn to feel safe, practice and allow it. Be open to the good and gratitude will naturally follow.

Realise that I changed "survivor" into "SURVIVED!"

"Survived" is past tense, "survivor" feels like it is still continuing on. It really isn't! I LOVE YOU! (If you need it! Well... I LOVE YOU, anyway.

I found an amazing woman on YouTube, "Anna Bey" that has really helped me in this area around money and learning to receive. She teaches women how to level up in society and bag a "rich man" or a richer man than they think they are worthy of.

When I first came across her, I was horrified but as I continued watching her videos and heard what she had to say, I couldn't help but agree with her.

If you're like how I used to be, and find receiving difficult, you can start with something simple, saying "thank you" in an open receiving way when a man, or anyone gives you a compliment.

I don't agree with everything Anna Bey says, I mention my disagreement in the "Feelings chapter", but she is an amazing human being like we all are. She has great life experiences and interesting views that many can learn from, especially if they often give too much of themselves to men and the men never give anything in return.

Sex: Good or Bad?

CHAPTER 16

Amsterdam

I went to Amsterdam with a partner I was in a long term committed relationship with. I felt safe and comfortable with him. I knew he loved me, and I knew he would do anything for me within reason to make me happy. I knew he only had eyes for me. I adored him and loved him to bits. I knew we were 100% committed to each other, and I felt safe, secure, and stable.

While we were in Amsterdam, we walked through the red-light district. I walked past many windows with a red glow light surrounding it. There were women in each of these windows and I knew what they were there for. Prostitutes.

Real, live, legal prostitutes. I walked past confidently with my man. Feeling happy that wasn't me and feeling happy that I had my one and only man that I planned to be with forever.

This was Amsterdam. This was normal. This was their life and their job and how they make a living. I wasn't going to judge it. I wanted to have a happy and joyful time. Even if it was against my soul, I wasn't going to shame anyone for their choices. Love and acceptance all around.

The soul is always love and acceptance, which I can't imagine is easy to feel when you do something like prostitution.

Walking past I only allowed myself to feel excited, not nervous, as I was experiencing a new city and what it was famous for and what tourists go for. I had heard so much about it and here I

Sex: Good or Bad?

was experiencing it in the flesh.

I mentioned to the man I was deeply committed to, and I knew was committed to me that I wanted to go to a sex show. I was super curious. When I said it, I felt dread in the depth of my stomach. I knew it was against all religions, and it wasn't good for anyone, but we were in a country where this sin was normal. I also knew that I carried a lot of shame with me, and I knew that many people outside of religions say that repressing your sexuality is harmful. I always had a lot of confusion around sex, was it good or was it bad? I wanted to experiment by watching a sex show. Make myself feel liberated and fun, out there, like many of the times I chose to have a one-night stand and had an enjoyable time when not expecting a relationship.

I was in a committed relationship with a man that I knew loved me. Could anything go wrong? Before we started queuing up my man said to me, "Are you sure you want to do this? You're not going to start going off on one, are you? You're not going to blame me if you don't like it?"

I did feel embarrassed having to strongly tell my partner that I did really want to go to this sex show, especially as I had told him porn was awful and not real sex and the women are abused, and it is not good for the world. This was the same.

I let my partner know that I wouldn't go off on one with him and I was 100% going to be cool.

We joined the back of the queue which wasn't terribly long and waited. I was nervous deep down but refused to acknowledge it. I had to do this as part of my healing journey or so I believed! I had to show myself there was nothing wrong or shameful about this. Feel liberated. The show was there legally and hundreds of people paid to see it every night.

The other people in the queue didn't have energy like mine. I judged them thinking they were nervous. Me projecting my nerves onto them. "What we see in others is a reflection of ourselves." I made eye contact and smiled at a lady that didn't look happy.

She didn't smile back at me and looked a bit glum; perhaps she was tired as it was after midnight, but I made the assumption that it was her partner's idea to go and see the show and she wasn't particularly keen.

In fact, many of the people in the queue for the show didn't seem enthusiastic or happy. Were they all nervous like I was? Did they feel bad about their actions underneath too?

We were all about to experience sex on a stage purely for our entertainment and not love. The people performing on the stage but also us audience members watching, zero love. Everyone in the queue was a pervert. I felt like a pervert deep down, but I was adamant I was going to add some love to it and not acknowledge the pervy part of me.

We were getting closer to the front of the queue, and I suddenly realised the posts holding the rope to divide the queue line up were big brass penises.

"Ha, ha. Look at this" I squealed in excitement. I stroked the cold metal up and down with my hand, thinking it was hilarious.

"That's the kind of energy we like here." The guy that was about to let us through said. It was going to be an experience.

Sex is normal and nothing people should feel ashamed about yet, deep down I had a dark niggling feeling that I had to push past. Let my love and light shine through instead, which I managed to do. I grinned at the guy, I am guessing he was security or something, he reached into the cashier's booth, pulled out a penis lolly, and gave it to me.

I giggled some more, thanked him, and showed it to my partner. I felt even more embarrassed deep down that I had drawn attention to myself in such a way. Everyone else in the queue looked solemn. I just found it quite strange to be so solemn when going to a sex show as if it was a completely normal thing to go and do.

"Perhaps this is just the norm for the others around me?" I

Sex: Good or Bad?

thought.

I guess I was judging these people. I always like to show good energy wherever I go. I guess these people were just being their normal selves and I was pushing myself to be happier.

"Maybe they are just bored of waiting?" I thought.

I didn't unwrap the lolly straight away. I felt slightly afraid to suck the penis shaped lolly in-front of the security guard. I didn't want him to get the wrong impression.

We had 2 drinks included with our ticket purchase and while my partner went to the loo, I got us some drinks and waited for him in a row of spare seats in the audience at the top by the stairs.

I watched a woman wearing a sexy lingerie set with suspenders, stockings, and heels, whipping a guy from the audience. He ended up bent over and having his trousers pulled down and the lady whipped him some more. The fact there were many of us in the audience made it seem like it was ok and acceptable, and no one was getting hurt.

In truth, it could have felt extremely uncomfortable to watch.

I was with my partner, and I felt safe being close to him. It was a bit violent, and violence can never be good for a world that experiences many horrors already, it just adds to it.

I was able to let myself not get triggered and just watched for the fun of it and see how healed I was on my journey of shame around sex.

I wasn't feeling anything, either I was healed or blocking it out, numb.

We saw many different acts; I will tell you about the specific acts I remember as I felt strong reactions from them.

Britney Spears' "Baby one more time" song came on and a lady was positioned on a chair in a sexy schoolgirl outfit. She did an amazing balancing position on the chair that I automatically cheered for and wanted to say well done to her. I wanted her to feel appreciated for something other than taking her clothes off and having sex.

No one else cheered. Of course, me being in my ego, was judging them and their energy being off and nothing like my bubbly joyful interacting self.

After she did a few more amazing poses and did a little dance, she came into the audience and picked out a guy to go up on the stage with her. She sat him down on a chair and straddled herself across his lap, with her back to the audience.

The music played and we all watched, wondering what was going to happen next. She took off her bra and threw it across the stage. She then did a little dance before turning to face the audience revealing her breasts to us. I cheered for her again.

She was a woman, a human being with a soul, and I wanted her to feel loved and never ashamed. Could I have been feeling ashamed?

The guy next to me, not my partner, the guy on the other side of me, caught on and he also cheered, it made me happy. I love being in the audience and being the first to clap and hearing the rest of the crowd follow. It is an exhilarating feeling. Like being the leader.

The topless lady then got the man to remove his shirt and lay down on the stage. I watched eagerly to find a moment to keep cheering her on and continue the positive vibe for her.

She took her knickers off and I remember seeing her shaven nakedness between her legs. I thought about how women, including myself, look vulnerable and sweet. No big scary bulge, just flat. It made me feel vulnerable too.

When I watched porn, I didn't have the same feeling.

I suppose cheering this lady on, in person and giving her love from my heart, I saw a real woman in front of my eyes. Not a lady on a screen.

The lady then got a pen or a lip stick; she removed the cap and I watched with love from my soul. I was now just quietly watching like the rest of the audience, about to see the next move. I was present. She looked me in the eyes, and I was smiling at them. I felt connected to my soul.

Unexpectedly, she then inserted the pen into her vagina. I suddenly felt deep shame coming up out of my eyes, from the pit of my stomach. I then saw darkness flashing from behind her own eyes and I immediately felt immense guilt that I hadn't been able to block out the truth from my soul.

My soul's reaction had in-turn ignited hers. I felt a deep responsibility and I felt terrible. I had just made her feel ashamed about what she was doing because I couldn't hide my own shame.

I then forced myself to find moments where I could start cheering for her again and show her some love and support. She of course carried on with her act and was then able to block out any feelings of shame.

Maybe I was projecting onto her, and maybe she was fine with this on a soul level. Perhaps the dark flash I saw behind her eyes was just her knowing that I had deep shame in me, and she had just felt bad for me for being in the audience, while she felt happy doing what she did. I can't tell you what the truth is for another, but I know what a dark flash behind the eyes is, deep dark and terrifying.

Perhaps the shame and pain only come from the judgement of others? Maybe there is nothing to feel ashamed about at all and the shame only comes from being ostracised for a choice that you made. Or when someone commits a crime against you and makes you keep quiet about it? Why would someone make someone keep quiet about it? Because the shame comes from deep within them, and they pass it on.

We continued to watch the acts that came on the stage before us. Real live people performing real live sex acts, pussy licking, cock sucking and intercourse!

The next act I remember vividly because I had a strong reaction to it, was a black male and female on stage physically having sexual intercourse.

You can imagine the humongous size of the black man's penis it being a sex show! It was ginormous! The black man was having sex with the woman, and he was going deeper and deeper inside her vagina; the stand they were performing the sex act on was spinning around and around and around, the music was getting intense, and he seemed to be getting a bit aggressive, "how far can my penis go into to her?"

He was really trying to go as deep as possible into her, just wanting to go in, no regard for the feelings of the woman. The woman had her hand across her face and my gut feeling was she wouldn't be enjoying that.

Suddenly I snapped, "Be gentle! You cunt!" I screamed in pure outrage. I couldn't help it!

I felt like I was being good, showing love, care and compassion for the lady. I was also extremely worried, as I peered over at the security guard to see if I was about to get thrown out for losing my temper.

Luckily, he wasn't looking at me and I was about to relax when my then partner butted in. "Don't shout like that. Be quiet. Calm down." I was about to calm down but then I felt annoyed at him for not being on my side and supporting my emotional outburst.

I shouted at him, "Don't tell me to calm down, what I am doing is a good thing! I am protecting her! If the security guard wants me to be quiet, he will tell me to be quiet!"

When I looked back at the stage the black man had stopped thrusting his dick into her so deeply and seemed to be being gentler. Even so, I still felt uncomfortable with the way I had reacted. What if I had got it wrong and the lady on stage was genuinely fine with what was going on?

I then thought that everyone in the audience including the security guard might have guessed about my shameful past. I felt exposed like everyone knew about me. I sat down and took a few breaths and got myself into the present moment and away from the embarrassing moment. At least I hadn't been thrown out for it.

Another act I remember because of my reaction was when the stage curtains were pulled apart and a white lady and a white man were in the doggy position. The man was spanking the woman's butt with a smirk on his face, as if he knew there was an angry woman in the audience.

The spanking of the woman made me feel uncomfortable, but I didn't want to react aggressively. I allowed this to happen however I was feeling about it.

It went on a bit more and the lady was trying to put on a brave laughing face for the audience. It looked fake to me.

Suddenly when I could take no more, I shouted out aggressively again, "slap him round the face!"

Shock horror had it that a male in the row behind me stood up and shouted too. "Stick it in her arse!"

My instinct was fuming mad and angry! My insides squirmed and I couldn't believe that this male shouted what he did. This was a real live woman on the stage, and he was shouting out like she was a piece of meat and getting off on watching this violence towards a woman.

Before I could even think if I wanted to retaliate, the security guard sternly said, "No shouting out!"

I had to sit with my uncomfortable feelings. I felt like a lot of the attention was now on me and not the couple on the stage.

I felt so uncomfortable that a male would happily see this real-live woman as a piece of meat. This type of man had left my consciousness and no longer existed in my world. I felt completely violated. I felt sad and powerless too.

When the couple left the stage, more acts came on.

We watched the rest of the show until the last act when it finished at 2am.

I had to use the loo before we left so I went upstairs to use it. On my way back down the stairs I passed a good-looking and toned muscular black guy. I smiled at him, and he nodded his head at me in return. I gazed at his physique appreciatively before making eye contact with him.

I suddenly froze in fear. I had a feeling it was the same black man from the stage earlier that I shouted at. I covered up my fear and shame and smiled at him sweetly. I could tell from our eye contact that he wasn't a bad man. Just a man. A man doing his job. I did wonder if I might have taught him something, by shouting at him on the stage. Did he know it was me?

Walking back through the red-light district, we passed a couple more ladies in the windows.

I was still aware of wanting to shine love and light to the women. I smiled at the ladies we walked past. One lady opened the door and told me she wanted me. I smiled my smile of love and joy at her. I was entertained but I also wanted her to feel loved.

I surrendered and continued to smile at her. "If you really want me," I said through my eyes.

"I want you both," she added, pointing at my partner.

My partner disagreed and was not keen. I was relieved as I hadn't really wanted to go in there. I knew my partner wouldn't go in there, but him confirming it was a relief.

She gave me a stern look. Was she a bit cross with me? I couldn't tell. She was the one that came out to me. All I did was smile to show some love to her. I think she was very closed off from any emotion. She was obviously just after money. It's funny because I remember seeing 2 different guys get practically thrown out of the doors by the women in there. The doors were slammed shut behind them, as if to say, "get out, not welcome here anymore!" They got their money and the man got whatever he thought he wanted.

However, walking past the glowing red windows and witnessing what I did... feeling into my soul where the truth lies... I would have felt sadness. Sad for the women and sad for the men that succumb to this. Sad for my past self that could have easily become like these women.

I have heard many times that prostitution is the oldest profession, however, are we in the cavemen times, animalistic/survival brain era or have we come a long way, and evolved a lot since those times? The lower brain or survival brain is active just for survival.

Having sex when not in love is totally against the soul's natural state which is love.

CHAPTER 17

Freedom or a Trap

My "Heavenly Experience" chapter already explains, what happened when I decided to go celibate.

However, even though that experience was out of this world and like no other, I wanted to share another lady's story.

Jessica's story

This was a good sexual experience as I felt empowered. I made the choice to break it and in the moment it was fantastic.

One of my best friends and I decided to have a night out with the two of us, dancing and having a few drinks. I was in my early to mid-twenties.

I decided to go all out and even put a few loose curls in my blonde hair with my curling wand. I felt pretty and dressed up which I hadn't done for a while. I was doing it for myself to feel good to have a girly night out with my friend. I had chosen to be celibate for a while and flirting with a man was the last thing on my mind.

However, while I was having a dance on the dance floor, a man came over to me and straight up asked me if I wanted to go back to his house with him.

At this point, I wasn't naïve, and I knew what he really meant. I knew what a random man in a nightclub would want with a pretty dressed up girl like me, to randomly go back to his house.

My first initial reaction was, "what the fuck?" It was a bit of a shock and I instantly thought "no way! Who does he think he is?" But I quickly changed my perspective. I didn't like to be aggressive. I pondered on the thought and then I eyed him up and thought he was quite attractive. I thought I might like to try this out.

I thought to myself that it had been a while since I had any attention and a quick one night where I felt in-control, might be fun, liberating, freeing. I wanted to feel free.

He had been straight-up honest with me in a language I understood. He hadn't tried to manipulate me or lie to me. I felt in control of the situation. The fact he asked me outright was intriguing too. Men don't usually do that. My belief was they try it on and then don't take "no" for an answer.

I realised he was a player type of man; he had a lot of experience sexually with women and found women easy. I didn't see him as good looking straight away but looking back he was definitely, better looking and attractive than a lot of other men I had experienced. I didn't feel any fear at all. I only felt excitement. I was allowing myself to let go and enjoy whatever was coming next. I said I wanted him to come to my place (I felt more in-control that way).

My daughter was away for the weekend, and no one was home. When I got home, I left him in the lounge to go upstairs and change into my sexy Ann Summers underwear. I wanted to feel as sexy and physically gorgeous and confident as I could to heighten the experience for both of us. He liked it. He took a deep breath and told me he wasn't expecting that. I guess I really was the one in control.

I felt free for a change, rather than holding myself back from feeling guilt and shame. We just went for it.

He was good and knew what he was doing and then I had an experience that I had never ever had before. I must have been having an orgasm, a different kind I hadn't had before, and my eyes were closed.

I decided to open my eyes to see where the guy had gone as I couldn't sense him near me. I was absolutely mortified at what I saw. A jet stream of water was shooting out from between my legs across the other side of the room.

"OH MY GOD!" I thought! "What the f**k is that. Is that pee? Am I peeing? How do I stop it?" I was absolutely mortified, and I had never even heard of female ejaculation before. I thought I wanted to stop it but then when I tried to stop, it meant holding back the good releasing feeling. I thought "F**k it" and I continued to allow this crazy happening to continue, it did feel liberating! I wasn't caring about the guy I had never met before in my bedroom. I was focusing on myself and what I wanted. I wanted wholesome fun and a liberating time, a release.

I most certainly did get a release, an embarrassing release I had never experienced before.

Looking back, I think he was shocked and not expecting that at all. I wasn't either.

Afterwards, he asked for my number, and I gave it to him. I wasn't expecting him to get in touch with me again. This time I didn't care. I knew what I was going in for and I did it. I wasn't expecting him to message me to come around again the next night. I was shocked but also excited. He liked me! Seeing a guy, a second time, meant that he really liked me. That is what I believed.

I suddenly felt excited that this could be the start of something special and romantic and I decided I liked him too. I felt nervous because my experience was when I liked a guy, it didn't work out. I had the crazy insecure worried feelings start to commence. I was remembering what happened the night before and I was wondering how I was going to match it. I was trying to think of ways to please him, rather than think about how I was feeling and what I wanted.

I thought a good thing to do would be to wear a different one of my sexy Ann Summers outfits underneath a dressing gown. I believed that is why he liked me and that is what he came around for, so that is what I was going to do.

The fact he was at my house for a second night in a row was good in my eyes. It wasn't going to be a one-night stand. This was potential for a relationship! All my excited nerves came in. I still hadn't learnt anything about men at this stage. All I ever knew is that I wanted love and romance and I had the looks to have a man to want me and love me.

The feelings I felt overtook me and all I could think of was how I got him to want to come back around. What had I done the night before? Sex with a sexy Ann Summers outfit.

That is what happened the night before because that is what I had wanted to happen, and I felt empowered and in control of myself and happy. I wasn't expecting any outcome of a relationship; because I had learnt from the past, sex didn't mean love and a relationship.

When he came around, I had my dressing gown covering my sexy outfit. I suddenly felt really awkward. I hadn't felt excited and free like I had done the night before, I felt uncomfortable and embarrassed.

After sitting on the sofa for a bit in an awkward silence, we did eventually go upstairs to my bedroom. I was relieved because I was uncomfortable and felt like I could only feel comfortable once we were in the act of sex.

Having sex meant I had all his attention and I believed he wanted me. I knew it was a gamble and after I felt ashamed because I hadn't felt free like I had done the night before. I was trying to please him and not please myself.

I felt like I was forcing myself to do it. No longer happy and free in the moment. When he left, the pining feeling came in. Pining for love and to have him around me. Wondering if he will call or text me again. I can't remember if I sent him a message again, a simple boring message to see if he would reply. If I did, he didn't reply, or it was even more simple and boring just to be polite to me and it would have stung me deeply because I knew he didn't want me for love.

Knowing what I know about men now, and how to behave around them, I completely understand where Jessica went wrong in this situation.

I am here to teach you from the mistakes I and others have made and how to do it differently if you ever found yourself in that situation. (Not that this book is encouraging anyone to go out and have one-night stands, or sex without love and commitment, but I do know it happens.)

The excitement and nerves took over when Jessica realised, he wanted to see her again.

Whether it was for sex or to see her and get to know her, what Jessica should have done was check in with where she was at and what she wanted. The excitement was because he wanted to see her again.

Why she was excited was because she thought it had the potential to develop into a relationship.

If she had control over her emotions and understood this alongside the understanding of men, she would have loved herself enough to make sure she took care of herself and her emotions.

Jessica should have been brave and brutally honest with herself and then been able to communicate that to him. When he asked for her number in the morning and said he would come back that night, she possibly had doubts. So, a part of her was testing him and when he did, she felt over the moon.

But what Jessica should have done was to have known what her boundaries were. Checked in with herself, what did she want?

She should have explained to him that she had an incredible night with him, and she would be keen to see him again, but she didn't feel comfortable with him going to her house again and she would feel much more comfortable meeting in a public place and have a proper date to get to know him like that.

If he was interested in getting to know her better, then she would have known and if he wasn't and only wanted to get in her knickers then she would have known that too.

At least she could have decided based on what she knew about men and how she felt about herself. Men are attracted to women and respect women that know what they want and can stick to their own guns and look after their own feelings. Of course, a lot of women think a man knows how they would feel, how they want to be treated etc.... but men are not mind readers, they need to be told in black and white.

When I see that my husband does whatever I ask of him, I know he really does love me and that is an extremely satisfying and content feeling to have; not to mention an extremely loving feeling and that makes me feel good to do whatever he wants me to do for him.

People are treated how they allow themselves to be treated, and most badly behaved people do feel bad about treating another poorly. They just can't help themselves because they feel far away from the truth of love and light from the source of creation, or God.

Even abusive people can be sorry after the violence they inflict but they always do it again because the victim feels unable to take themself away from that situation.

We will never know if the tools Jessica has now would have

worked on this man after she had sex with him because right from the start, he made it clear he wanted to have sex with her.

I don't think he was expecting Jessica to agree when she did. The problem was after her night of freedom, she got attached. When he showed interest in her again, she got excited and wanted a relationship.

If Jessica had still felt in control of herself and her feelings, felt them and expressed them; if she had told him she didn't want to have sex again however good it was unless he was willing to form a committed relationship with her; knowing what I taught her she would have protected herself, knew how she felt and kept herself safe by not wanting to please him in the situation, and making sure she took care of herself, she would have seen if he went along with it, then it could have become a relationship.

However, if he had just left her and not asked for her number or gone to see her again, which is what she was expecting to happen, a free, fun, liberating one night stand, she could have handled that. When she agreed to have sex, she knew exactly what she was letting herself in for, she was prepared until she thought he liked her.

Jessica says "of course, it is never a fulfilling feeling afterwards, always empty, lonely, but never any proper hurt feelings because I knew in advance. I wasn't expecting anything from him, no relationship or any kind of attention, I guess that is why I could feel so liberated and free at the time of intercourse with the stranger."

I remember reading an article in a magazine about a lady that went to swinging clubs. She said that one day she saw a man on a train that she recognized and realized that she had been intimate with him at one of these events.

She explained how ashamed she felt and that she would never go to another one of those events ever again.

Sex: Good or Bad?

CHAPTER 18

Slut

How would you describe the word slut?

Most often you think of a woman. A woman that has sex with multiple people. It is most often seen as a shameful word.

I was having a conversation with a friend the other day and she was gossiping about a woman that she didn't like. She was going into details about how she was sleeping with one of her friends and she was telling me how she cheated on someone and "keeps opening her legs."

She told me she'd had words with her and made her cry. I had to butt in and explain to her that it is ok to cry. It is actually particularly good to cry. Everyone has feelings and should cry if they feel the need to. She told me it was the truth that made her cry.

I said to her that she was very lucky not to understand her pain and torment. I don't understand why she would want to revel in this woman's pain of making her cry because she is a "slut" and doesn't like her behaviour. Why care so much with negativity about someone else's private affairs?

The truth is being deeply intimate with someone shouldn't ever become gossip. Sex with someone is meant to be private and between two consenting partners. It is a form of love in that precise moment and should remain private between the two. It is not for the entertainment of others. Whatever the reason for either of the consenting parties reasoning to have sex. It is up to each individual to make whatever decision they want to do.

Also, some men seem to think if one man has sex with a woman, then they can try and have a go too. That is not fair on the woman to be hit on for sex when she should be protected in order to feel safe.

This is an example of someone else's behaviour causing grief in another. If someone's "slutty" behaviour causes stress in you, I invite you to ask yourself why? Why does it make you feel a certain way? How can you feel better about it? Find a deeper understanding of why a woman would act like a "slut" and realise that someone else's sex life shouldn't have even reached your ears!!

I was shamed a lot in my adolescent years, and it has stayed with me forever since. No one understood why I was behaving like I did and being shamed and hated by some made it an extremely distressing time. I was already feeling deep shame and to think that people were discussing it was horrendous.

I was always good at covering up my real feelings around it, as I never let myself cry about it. I didn't know I was doing anything "bad" or "shameful", if a man came onto me (depending on the man) I felt flattered as I didn't have a very good opinion of myself and I gave him what he wanted quite easily. It was attention, attention that I badly craved because I didn't feel worthy. Friends were in disbelief at what I did when I was incredibly young.

My ego liked the shock factor of it and getting my name around. My ego wanted to be known and didn't see anything wrong in my behaviour.

When I realised a lot of men didn't take no for an answer when they heard I was "easy" and a "slut", I found it even easier to just get it over with quickly. Then I wanted to take control of the situation and put myself in situations where I was the one that chose to do the "slutty" actions. When I got shamed a lot for it, it hurt deeply as all I wanted was love and connection. It was the only way I knew how but then my toxic ego just wanted to cover up any pain rather

Slut

than address it. Feeling the pain and shame and releasing it.

I am grateful that I was "slut" shamed because if I hadn't been, then I may never have chosen to be celibate and wait for the one to marry me. I could have taken a completely different path and never experienced the beautiful spiritual experiences I did have.

Even though still, I have love and compassion for the women that believe they are happy being free and doing as they please. Desperate for love like most of us are but unable to experience it due to negative beliefs from past experiences and past experiences of others.

Even though after going celibate and many times, I had it ripped away from me, (sometimes by my own choice) the cycle would repeat itself, so what was the point?

Another reason the woman would cry by being confronted for her actions is because she was completely unaware that her actions would cause disgust in another.

Just as I never knew it would cause disgust in another. She wanted love and connection and knew that her actions weren't creating it with the partner, but when other onlookers had a negative opinion, it was even more of a disconnection and lack of love feeling, especially from a woman, wouldn't a woman understand?

My view is that the women who are unkind to "sluts" are very insecure themselves and are probably afraid to have their own man be led astray by one. Instead of taking responsibility for not getting a man completely devoted to her, and understanding nature and men in general, they want to blame the other woman.

In my experience the unfaithful woman is lied to by a man already in a relationship, just so he can get have his ego inflated and possibly get a need met he is not getting met at home.

When I got older, I chose to stay alone and block everyone out, and not think that people would gossip about me even if they

137

did.

Partly due to deep shame but also due to fear.

I couldn't even make new friends because of the shame I felt. If they found out they would never want to be my friend.

My abusive ex that drummed it into me that I was a slut and no one else would want me because of it, that didn't help the deep shameful feelings I had. If I was that awful for the past men I was with, then why was he so keen to want to be with me?

He made me feel ashamed where I didn't want to have sex with him. Although when he finally cheated on me, he then said one of the reasons he liked me in the beginning was because of the sex.

Dearest men!! If you like the sex with a particular woman, never ever make her feel ashamed or she will stop wanting sex with you! It damages her for future relationships too!

Not feeling like I had any friends led me on to seeking out other connections, taking whatever came my way and hoping it would lead onto the relationship I wanted but didn't think I deserved or was too afraid it would turn abusive.

At the back of my desperate mind thinking "I might as well get paid money for doing what I do. I have the looks. Some women get paid thousands of pounds!"

I turned to God in deep times of need and I ended up having many incredible experiences, when going celibate, some of which I write about in this book.

When you become spiritually enlightened you don't care about gossiping about other people. I stopped gossiping a long time ago and avoid partaking in it. If you're unaware or unaware of the power some call God. You can feel afraid and get sucked back into doing it. I do have moments where I find myself getting sucked into it though. I am still far from perfect.

I also knew the pain of it when, you know deep down people talk about you behind their backs.

Consciously choosing not to partake in low vibe discussions and choosing love, compassion and understanding, really helps you on the path of experiencing glimpses of God's purity. Only Gods' pure love exists."

I read the following from "A course in Miracles":

"Perfect love casts out fear,

If fear exists,

Then there is not perfect love.

But:

Only perfect love exists,

If there is fear,

It produces a state that does not exist."

Sex: Good or Bad?

CHAPTER 19

Tantra

Scrolling through my Facebook page I came across a post on Tantra, written by a woman. It was a professionally written powerful post, thought and feeling provoking. It struck a deep chord in me.

I cannot say I disagree with the post at all, in fact once upon a time I would have been seriously passionate about the post, feeling anger and rage and agreed with it 100% even sharing it on my own Facebook page for all my Facebook friends to read.

I still 100% understand the post but I cannot go against Tantra either. I have my own viewpoint on it.

The writer was talking about Tantra and had her own experiences of it and her viewpoint. There were also a few thousand comments agreeing with her and some saying how she expressed the words to what they were feeling. There was a 14-year-olds piece of artwork too and the mum asked if she could use the words, to go with her painting.

The painting was of a naked woman being prodded and poked around. Her hand on her throat with blood and lots of blood around her uterus area. It was dark.

The first line used the words "Misogynistic Patriarchal Tantra" to describe the Tantra that they must have experienced to be able to write such a powerful and passionate post. It felt amazing to read, and it struck me deep at the core of my being. But knowing what I know now about men and women often being at war with each other, I have another viewpoint on it.

The post was saying how Tantra never teaches women boundaries, or how to say "no" it teaches women to submit and surrender.

Be open, feminine, and beautiful. It says when a woman is angry, Tantra tells her to calm herself down as anger is not spiritual or loving. She should smile. Tantra doesn't want her to say "no", Tantra says she should be open and loving and if she is not then it is called "wounds with the masculine and she should work on it and heal". The post goes on to say they strip the woman of all her fierceness to protect herself.

"They filed down her fangs, clipped her claws, pried open her legs and then sold her back to you as the Goddess."

Such an amazingly powerful read but obviously I can't publish it as it would be copying it; but you get the gist of it.

Well, what can I say?

After reading such an amazing powerful post that I cannot disagree with at all. I must tell you Tantra is good. Tantra is amazing and incredible, but a woman should only submit and surrender when a man has given her the 100% commitment she deserves and has made her feel safe to submit and surrender.

When I first met my husband, I believed I was quite mean to him. Obviously, I can't have been that mean to him, because he kept suggesting that we meet up and buying me dinners and drinks and wanting to take me out.

I had my angry mode up, "who does he think he is? Keep taking me for dinners!"

At the back of my mind, he was trying to soften me up to sleep with me. That is what I believed, and I refused to let it work!

However, I never said "no" to the dinners, as he was Muslim and I had reverted to Islam and I wanted to complete half my deen, which is half the religion, do certain things to complete your deen while in this life, to please God and enter heaven in the afterlife.

Getting married was half of it and I was adamant that I was going to get married. I was not even that keen on him in the beginning, but I wasn't keen on meeting any other Muslim men either.It was either, don't be a Muslim and find someone else (which I really didn't want to do) or stick with the religion and do right by Allah/God (which is what I was really keen to do).

I really wanted to be married and I really didn't think I would find anyone to marry me. I didn't have the confidence to tell them exactly what I wanted, which was marriage as I had a belief it might scare them away and it was better to have someone around than to scare them away. I now know that is ridiculous and if a man is scared away by wanting to give his fullest commitment, then let him get as far away as possible!

I am sharing my experience to help others.

In the beginning, I felt I was quite rude at times but really, I was having strong boundaries. I felt I was rude and mean because I was used to not having any boundaries up at all, but I knew he was a Muslim man and I knew that his religion, getting married is important so I felt safe being a bit mean with my reasoning behind it.

It wasn't easy because he did a lot of things I didn't like, and I found disrespectful. It was quite stressful. But I kept being "mean" and over the top and fierce. He even admitted that I was "scary." It didn't stop him from messaging me and still wanting to meet up though. I felt like a hard woman with my "claws out".

Surprise surprise, we're now married. I love him dearly because he showed me true respect and love by marrying me. I submit and surrender to him most of the time, but I still remember my boundaries and how I feel.

I often am a bit too laid back as it is easier and what I was always used to being like. If I start to feel bad about something, I start kicking up a fuss, and he shows me true love and he does what he can to make me feel better. It's hard work but worth it. I often make sure I don't abandon myself and keep loving myself. I make sure I don't lose myself in him and I take time out for myself when I need to.

When I don't feel too loving towards him and have built up resentment; I take time out and then when I come back, I am able to express it and he always makes me feel better. He is a diamond gentleman!

Tantra is good if you first learn to have boundaries and say "no" and always say "no" and be the "fierce" woman with claws, if that is how you feel.

Self-respect comes first but submitting and surrendering and saying how you feel when you feel safe works like magic too.

On my journey of researching and wanting to get a man to commit to me, I downloaded an E-book full of psychology tips and tools It was "Obsession Phrases" by Kelsey Diamond.

I found it quite terrifying when I learnt what the film director had been doing to me to get exactly what he wanted. I never had the heart to want to do it myself to someone. Occasionally I would slip out a phrase if it was an honest phrase. Giving compliments, I can't remember exactly everything in it as it wasn't my favourite information resource to use. It felt manipulating and cruel.

However, I learnt about the "push, pull" tactic to get the man hooked. It recently came to me that when you have strong firm boundaries when you genuinely feel you need to have them, you are naturally "pushing" them away, and when you feel safe to be open, vulnerable, authentic, and expressing yourself, or being fun, playful and feeling free, you're inviting them in or "pulling" them towards you.

I do think the terrifying psychology E-book I read, all women and men should learn about it so they're aware. Not to manipulate others, but so they are aware if others are doing it to them.

It is a proper head-fuck, and I am shocked at what I read!

Sex: Good or Bad?

CHAPTER 20

Baby

I was 17, or 18 when I was sitting in the YMCA listening to an Eminem CD and hearing the lyrics,

"Sometimes I sit, staring out the window, watching this world pass me by, sometimes I think there's nothing to live for, I almost break down and cry, sometimes I think I am crazy, I am crazy oh so crazy, why am I here? Am I just wasting my time? But when I see my baby, suddenly I am not crazy! It all makes sense when I look into her eyes."

I had never felt such a longing in my heart to have my own little baby. I saw a way out of my prolonged suffering; to have my very own bundle of joy and love. I sat and thought long and hard. I knew that I would need a man that would also want a baby. Even though I didn't care too much about that part, I was just adamant that I did not want to be seen as the stereotypical young single mother on benefits. I was already on benefits.

Most importantly I did not want to be seen as a "slag" or a" slut" or any other name to suggest that having sex with a boy or more than one boy and giving them what they wanted was to feel ashamed about.

I knew those names were already being said about me as many of those names I had already been tormented with before. I understand now, guys don't like women to be easy as it takes them away from their hunting game. Takes away their feeling of working hard to achieve something.

Sex: Good or Bad?

So, I did. When I was still a teenager, I remember feeling the desperation of wanting a baby. That is what sex is for, to procreate, so maybe it was my body's natural reaction to all the sex and all the different sperm. Or the empty feeling of all the oxytocin and feel-good sex chemicals but no result of nature's intentions from having sex.

Most likely I felt empty, unloved and used and abused and desperate for love. Having a baby would be the answer. I could feel all the love in the world for my very own little baby.

Many women do lead successful fulfilling lives without a baby, their work being their baby, but I didn't have anything. I religiously took my contraceptive tablets because there was no way I wanted to get pregnant with a random guy. The thought terrified me. Even though I wasn't in a relationship, I always seemed to end up having sex with a man anyway and worrying about getting pregnant or needing the morning after pill.

I was mostly terrified from the stigma and judgements of others, especially my family. All though looking back, I do think choosing a random guy would have been a better option than the situation I ended up in.

Longing for a baby, I knew that I wasn't going to get "up the duff" by any random guy even if I didn't care about being in a relationship to have a baby. I knew my baby would need a father.

All children need a good decent father figure in their life. I was also concerned about my age and being too young and how my parents would react. Even though I was living alone in the YMCA, I still cared what they thought of me. The thought of them knowing I had sex was too shameful to think about.

Two or Three years later, on my 20th birthday, mid-August, I moved into a maisonette through a housing association. I never called it a council flat because that was too degrading, even though I had been to the council asking for a place, because lo and behold,

Baby

I was pregnant!

My then partner had come with me and every few weeks and we would go into the council office, and he would not stop going on and on and on in an entitled way about how I needed it.

I am the sort of person to sit and wait patiently, but not him. If he wanted something he wouldn't stop going on about it. He was aggressive too and always had to have his own way. Looking back, I think it did help to quicken getting me the security of a permanent home that my baby and I needed.

My baby was due the day after my birthday. I was excessively big and had gained a lot of weight, not just from being pregnant but from overeating and not exercising too. I only had one outfit that I could wear. My mum had kindly bought it for me. I didn't particularly like it, a bright green 2 piece, ¾ length baggy trousers with a big panel covering my enlarged stomach, and a matching top. Even so, I was very grateful that I had clothes to fit me that I could wear out.

I was pregnant in the summer of 2006. That was the year the government banned people from using their hose pipes because it had been so hot and dry. The weather stayed warm into the early autumn too. I felt more comfortable at home, wearing minimal clothes, my maternity bra, and large comfy knickers.

One evening, a few days after moving into my very own apartment, I decided to leave the lounge where my baby's father was watching TV and go upstairs to my new baby's room.

My Granny had recently gone into a home, and I was given a lot of her furniture, so there was her guests single bed in the room with the cot and Moses' basket.

I sat on the bed and started to get comfortable. I was partly ecstatic and over the moon with joy at the thought of meeting my baby. I had put in a lot of effort to make sure we had everything.

Sex: Good or Bad?

We bought something every week with my then partners money to make sure he didn't throw it away in the bookies. I also made sure we had enough gas and electric and plenty of food to last until the next pay day.

I was living on eggshells wondering if one week we wouldn't have money to live on or to buy our baby what he needed.

I was constantly anxious and nervous each week if he would waste his money in the bookies or not. That is what most of the arguments we had were about.

The arguments escalated out of control and Bernard would smash glasses or punch walls. Once he punched my arm and left a deep bruise on it. I was pregnant with his child, and I was desperate not to be a stereotypical single mother on benefits. I couldn't leave. I wanted my baby to have a family. Mum and Dad. I certainly didn't want to be known as the evil female that stopped her child from seeing their father.

Sitting on the bed in my almost ready-to-be born baby's room, I was excited because any day I would meet my bundle of gorgeousness. I could love hard and deeply and provide everything my little baby would need, with government assistance of course that many people often like to make you feel guilty about.

At the time, all I could think of was cherishing and adoring my gorgeous little baby. I had no guilt then; I was just completely focussed on my baby.

We had everything my baby could possibly need. We had a giraffe change mat, with a matching hooded baby towel, a matching wash bowl and baby bath. Muslin cloths: I saw mums use them when their baby was sick, but it turned out I never needed to use a muslin cloth for that purpose.

We had the cot bed and the mattress. We had everything for my little love. All the money went towards our baby.

Baby

I couldn't wait to use all the new baby stuff and meet my baby, but on the other hand I had a sense of deep gloom.

When I moved into the new place, it felt like a fresh start and when the baby would be with us it would be a brand-new era for both Bernard and I to enjoy. I didn't think we would have any more arguments. What was there to argue about? We had a lovely new home, and our baby would almost be with us.

Bernard still had his flat, which felt good to me. It felt good that we had separate homes. Even though I wanted things to look good from the outside, I really wanted to be free of him.

"Kimberly!" (Is the character's name in my film script) I heard Bernard's voice call my name, as I heard his footsteps get closer. He sounded normal. I didn't think he sounded in a bad mood, so I just felt indifferent. I felt tired and heavy. Tired, heavy, and drained. I felt OK with the pregnancy up until the due date, but when it passed, it felt like there was no sign of the baby coming. I really wanted to meet the baby, have a cuddle, and feel what it would be like to be a nurturing nursing mother... but it felt like it was taking forever to come to light.

"Did you just walk past the window?" Any joy I had about the baby coming, left me. "Is he really going to start this now?" I thought.

I couldn't handle another argument. We argued before, when I was in temporary accommodation. He said people outside could see me and I was disgusting and shameful to stand near the window without clothes on.

I was in my underwear again and yes; I had just walked past the window. He was going to start yelling at me and draining me again.

I had no energy to stick up for myself, I broke down into tears, crying. In the beginning I thought he would see how upset I was, and if he loved me then surely, he would stop and have some sort of pity? He never did that though. He hated it when I cried. Looking back, I think he enjoyed it. (I have wondered if abusive men like to make women cry because it is the only emotion/feeling they can get out of her?)

Sitting on my bed, the physical heavy tiredness transmuted into mental heavy tiredness, "not again" I dreaded. I just wanted peace.

I started crying because I couldn't take anymore, "not now", I was exhausted and needed to muster up my energy for the gruelling labour I knew I had ahead of me, any day.

I had no one around me to love me with the baby that I couldn't wait to have and show so much love and adoration to. I felt like I was helpless.

"What are you crying for, you little slag?" Bernard bellowed. I couldn't take it; I cried even harder knowing it wouldn't make a difference to how it made him behave towards me. I had no idea it would result in his next action. I was taken by complete surprise.

He grabbed me around the throat and squeezed. I didn't really know what was happening until I was choking and couldn't breathe. I thought he might let go after a while but soon realised he wasn't going to. I had no way to punch or kick him off, as he was behind me.

The room around me started to go distant, as the pressure in my head felt expanded. "This is it." I thought. "I'm going to die." A deep wave of sadness washed through me as I realised wasn't going to get to meet my baby.

I turned to God. The greatest power that I always turned to in my time of desperation. This time I wasn't desperate. This time I was sorry and hoped he would let me into heaven. I apologised for all the sins I had ever committed in my life; I asked for forgiveness. I gently pleaded with him to make sure that my baby would be ok. All I felt was a tremendous amount of love moulding into the deepest sadness that I wouldn't be able to show this love to my baby.

As I accepted my destiny, I closed my eyes, surrendered, and let my body go limp, I felt my body being laid back onto the bed.

He did let go. I started crying hysterically. Then he said in a tone of voice that made me sound like I was over-reacting, "What? I wasn't going to kill you!"

I am not so sure; he wasn't letting go of my neck until I had totally surrendered.

I was alive and I did get to meet the most precious thing in my life. I loved having only my baby to worry about. I loved loving my baby with my whole heart.

Once I finally got rid of Bernard and was a single mum it was one of the best times of my whole life! Just me and my sweet baby, free from any negativity or a harmful man. (That is when I wasn't being harassed and verbally abused by Bernard through text messages and phone calls. I was happy to not have him physically around in our space).

Sex: Good or Bad?

CHAPTER 21

Forced sex. Report it!

The first time I decided I wanted to go celibate, I was 17 years old. I had been sectioned under the mental health act and I had been in the hospital for 3 weeks.

During my time before being admitted and afterwards, I was terrified. I had all kinds of crazy hallucinations and thoughts, and I was acting very strange, because I was terrified.

I'd had a bad mental reaction after a night of taking drugs with some acquaintances from the street. During my time in the hospital, I turned to God after finding a bible on my bedside table.

I was terrified and turning inward to the deepest part of myself that connected to God, I vowed that I would be good. I made a pact that I wouldn't be bad; do drugs, drink alcohol, be violent or have sex ever again.

It only lasted a couple of months before I was drinking again and going into the pubs. With my friend that lived in the YMCA with me, on a night out a man that was bad news took a liking to me.

I had been drinking and he followed us back to the YMCA. My friend told me I must not talk to the man, and I must go to my room.

However, when I was in my room, my buzzer went off, it was the man, 26 years old, almost a decade my senior.

When he asked me to go downstairs to talk to him, I naively followed his instructions.

Sex: Good or Bad?

I didn't want to have sex with him, but I did like the attention he was giving me. I had felt alone, and this was a bit of excitement.

When I was at the door, he asked me to go around the corner down the dark street with him. I kept telling him "No" and to talk to me where I was. He wasn't interested in doing so.

I felt curious and naïve as to what he wanted to tell me, and I did follow him down the dark street next to the YMCA building. He came onto me strongly and I kept telling him "No" but forcefully he managed to pull off my jeans. I just went along with it after that and let him have sex with me.

I kept trying not to have sex with him but like many others before him, he wouldn't accept my "no."

When he realised, I was going along with him, he took me home with him in a taxi. If I had been more virginal and sex wasn't something that excited me, if I hadn't had all the sexual experiences that I already had; I realise now that what he did to me was actually rape.

I ended up in something that I expected to be a relationship. In my head, we had had sex, so what we had was in fact a relationship. It wasn't a relationship; he was using me for sex.

At the time I felt scared to be in his presence. I thought it was because I liked him and he excited me, but looking back, I was afraid, and afraid with good reason to be.

He would ring my buzzer with a movie he had got from Blockbuster, and I hadn't experienced that before, I thought he was doing something good.

A £3 movie was nothing for him to get free sex from me. I was always so quiet and shy around him. Painfully shy because I wasn't comfortable. Because I didn't want to have sex and he didn't take my "no" for an answer.

I thought I loved this man and I thought we had something. My friend in the YMCA eventually told me that he had a fiance that he lived with.

My entire world came crashing down. The love fantasy I had created for myself wasn't real. I felt an excruciating pain. I wasn't going to let him get away with it. My other friend told me she used to work in the hairdresser with her, and she told me her new place of work.

I wrote his fiancé a letter. I had so much hatred and anger coming up to the surface, I hated him for doing what he did to me. I took the letter to her workplace and handed it to another shop assistant that could pass it on to her for me.

My anxiety was through the roof, I felt so afraid, a burning sensation pricked my skin all over, my cheeks felt flushed, but I was adamant not to let him get away with it.

As well as all of that, I felt powerful. I felt powerful and like I was taking control. The letter explained that I hated him when I found out about her. I wanted him to stay far away from me and never see him again. It also explained how angry I felt and that I wanted to smash her car up but of course I realised that it was him, not her I was angry at. I felt so much pain. I felt my pact with God had been destroyed and my soul burned as if it was on fire.

I gathered that the rapist man, my fantasy boyfriend, would get the message and stay away from me. I didn't hear from him for some time, and I felt happy and free and in-control.

One day, after three weeks my buzzer went off. I answered it, curious and excited that I might have a friend. It was him. My gut dropped. Any power I believed I had disappeared. I was at his mercy before he had even asked me if he could come up and see me.

My soul screamed, "Nooooooo!" I was frozen in fear. I didn't know how to listen to my soul at that point in my life.

I hadn't learned how to listen to my own being that knew what was good for me. I didn't know how to say "no" to a man. In my experience saying "no" to a man didn't work. I had no boundaries,

Sex: Good or Bad?

I was weak.

There was a little part of me that hoped that he was going to make the pain disappear and somehow, by some miracle, make my Disney romance dream become a reality.

I was curious as to what he wanted to say to me. I didn't learn from my past mistake, and I went downstairs to let him in. You can guess what happened next.

I ended up allowing him to rape me. He wanted me to sit on the bed next to him, which I did. He then laid his whole thick and heavy body on top of me, so I was unable to move. I didn't respond sexually this time. I knew I didn't want it. I definitely didn't want sex with him when I knew he had a partner.

I lay still, looking at the ceiling in a daze knowing that what he was doing wasn't good.

When he had finished, he told me to stay there and that he would let himself out. He left me feeling confused and empty. I had never cried about being raped before, but this was different. I made the decision not to respond sexually to him. I was adamant I wasn't going to allow my body to physically respond to him cheating on his partner. I knew that was wrong.

This time, I went to the part of me that had feelings, I felt the despair and I released it. I cried. I didn't care who heard me. I knew that you were supposed to talk about stuff like that and not keep it bottled up and I never had felt my true feelings around that before.

I cried hysterically until my friend came to me. She asked me what was wrong, and I just said one word. I said his name. She did what she could to comfort me, but she was 6 months younger than me, she was just a kid too.

Kids don't know what to do in that situation. Many adults don't either. I don't know if she knew what he had done. I never told anyone in words, but I did allow myself to feel what needed to be felt to be released. I cried.

Forced sex. Report it!

I started to feel angry and revengeful. I started to have thoughts of wanting to hurt him, kill him even, but my time in the hospital stopped me. I wanted to be good.

I was desperate not to have these thoughts and I was desperate to make sure I didn't act out in violence. I was desperate. I went to the deep place inside myself that connects to God, I begged God and I explained the bad thoughts I had and the bad actions I felt I wanted to do. I told God I just wanted to be good and to not hurt anyone, ever, because I wanted to be good. Good for him and to please him. I then asked God to send him to prison, so I was safe not to commit my own crime.

The next morning, my dear friend told me that he had gone to prison. I looked at my friend in total awe of God's amazement.

Her next sentence horrifies me to this day. "He went to prison for raping a fourteen-year-old girl." I think I disappeared into my soul; everything seemed far away. Still, I didn't say anything. But I think she knew what my tears were from.

I always wonder, if I had known to report him for his crime, if I had the support and knowledge of what to do, I always wonder if I would have saved the fourteen-year-old girl. Sometimes, I wonder if it was my fault, because of me he thought he could get away with doing it to someone else.

To me, the rape I had experienced was only normal. When in family therapy, one of my parents had described the sexual abuse I experienced as a child as "a normal part of growing up."

I never went into details about the abuse, but in my diary that the nurses read with me, I wrote, "he was always horrible to me, unless he wanted something however much, I didn't want to." The nurse then guessed. I guess I wrote it for that reason, desperate for help, but I was not expecting them to pass the information on to anyone else. I was 15 when I wrote in my diary, if I had waited a few months until I was 16, they wouldn't have had to tell my parents.

I was horrified and I then wrote in my diary that I made it all

Sex: Good or Bad?

up. I was desperate for it to be kept a secret. They didn't believe me, and I was made to sit in family therapy and be told it was a normal part of of growing up by someone that was supposed to care for me.

If enough people talk about this like it is normal, because it happens a lot, to some people many times, if everyone is taught at an early age to report it, there is more of a chance to save someone else from experiencing the trauma too.

The story I just wrote about with the 26-year-old, when I was 17, it happened so many years ago, but it often comes up in my memories now. I am in the process of erasing them for good, and to lead a life that is not full of fear.

I never reported the incident, I didn't know how. I didn't think it was a crime to be reported. If I did, I didn't think to report it, it wasn't in my conscience to report it. Over the years after experiencing other abuse from other men I did pluck up the courage to report some other incidents.

However, recently when I was on a night out, in the taxi queue at the bus stop, I noticed the young lady next to me was crying. She was with two friends, and I knew something wasn't right.

Her two friends were trying to get an answer out of her, as to why she was crying. She wasn't speaking to them.

I had my suspicions and I sat closer to her with an open heart and genuine care because I was worried about her, I don't like seeing people sad. My energy was kind, caring, understanding and gentle, knowing exactly how it feels and knowing how you can't speak of such crimes.

I asked her tactfully, coming from a place of non-judgemental, non-anger, total understanding, and gentleness,

"Did a man touch you?" Her eyes told me the truth as she continued to cry. I tried to tell her friends, "A man touched her!"

The bolder one quickly replied, "She hasn't said that. She

didn't say that!" I felt pushed away and turned away from trying to help their friend. The whole scene around me became distant as they weren't interested in listening. They did not want to believe the horrifying truth that happens too often and feels unspeakable.

She was trying to force out the reason why her friend was crying. The way she was, no way that she would have been able to communicate what had happened.

I felt my own voice being shunned away. I knew the truth and I was trying to help the crying girl still in her teenager years. I didn't know how. I was helpless. I at least needed her friends to listen to me.

Again, the girl looked at me with her eyes telling me that what I had said was true. I felt sad and helpless. What could I have done? Shouted at the loud girl trying to force the information out of her traumatised friend.

That would have made the girl feel afraid and may have triggered more aggression out of her friend. I didn't know how to help her.

In my head, I wasn't even thinking about calling the police. Would I have done that if she was able to speak her truth?

I couldn't call the police because the girl hadn't spoken about what happened.

However, the way her friend was trying to get the information out of her, was not the way to do it. If only, it was seen as more widespread and common, girls that randomly cry on a night out would automatically be asked by everyone, including her friends. "Did a man touch you?"

All she would have had to have done was to say "yes" or even just nod her head. Then the next step would have been to suggest to her that the best thing to do would be to call the police. Carefully and tactfully. Kindly and gently. Making her feel safe. Making her feel like it was the right thing to do. Letting her know that she has people by her side and not going to leave her. Then the bastard could have been caught. The police could have arrested him. Got him charged and convicted, and known to the police to watch him, to keep others safe.

Reporting crimes against people needs to be seen as the norm. Seeing sexual assault when it happens is important and necessary, so you can report it instantly. Everyone needs to talk about it more openly and widely. Perry Power teaches that being made to keep silent and then keeping silent is the trauma. Carries the deep shame when there needs to be none.

What she was wearing! She was wearing a short slinky white strappy dress. It sounds terrible that I saw what she was wearing and knew what the tears were from. It broke my heart. She would have felt pretty in that dress and then had it all stripped away from her.

She was so young. When I was that young, I didn't understand men. Not taught about men, I know now that men are visual and attracted to naked ladies, and they need sex more than a woman does. I also know that too many men can't control themselves and like to control women.

I learnt that men rape as an act of control. So, I wonder what goes through an abusive mans' head on a night like that one when I saw the crying lady in the bus stop.

"She looks vulnerable and sweet in that revealing dress. I will touch her. How dare she feel confident wearing a dress like that?"

Is that it? Their friends must learn to call them out on such behaviour if they witness it!

I know that some men don't think a woman should be allowed to dress up for herself, in a way she wishes to. Too many men feel entitled to a woman's body.

Men that think like this must learn about their ego, and what destroys the love and connection that we all need.

CHAPTER 22

Twin Flame Hell part 1

I dressed myself up one day in a long black elegant dress with a few sparkles that hugged my sexy curves perfectly. The split up the side of it let glimpses of my tanned and toned legs be shown. I teamed it with gorgeous diamanté heels, I curled my blonde hair and applied make-up to my face.

I felt like a million dollars, and I was excited to be going to an event with Z list "celebrities" and a red carpet. I had seen one of the "celebrities" before on one of the events' flyers on social media. I was instantly attracted to his photo. His face, his hair, I didn't think I was attracted to men with muscles and 6 packs, but I was instantly attracted to him. I felt a rush of euphoria looking at him.

I didn't think I would ever get him to notice me, but I was adamant to have a fun day and let go of any fears and insecurities. I knew whenever I had strong feelings for a guy and fancied them it never came to fruition, never ever, and all I would feel is extreme pain either from a painful rejection or from being used.

When I first noticed him, my insides squealed in delight like an excited teenage girl. I fancied him like crazy. I was terrified of how I felt because I knew if I allowed it to overwhelm me, attracting him would never come to fruition. I knew I had to not care about attracting him. I focussed on letting go of attachment thoughts to him and enjoyed the moment I was in.

It was more important for me to enjoy myself and not feel shy or embarrassed around him. I knew how I needed to feel within, if

Sex: Good or Bad?

I was going to have any chance of attracting him. I enjoyed feeling good and in the flow. Focussing on myself and feeling good, feeling free, letting go of any fear that he might think badly of me if he saw me.

It was ecstatic not caring what he thought of me. I was going to feel free of the fear and have an incredible time. I knew I didn't need him. I had already come far in life without him.

At one point my courage grew. I felt a bit naughty and thought I would try a little bit of flirting. I still did not think that he would ever be interested in me or give me any sort of attention.

I was free.

However much I was physically attracted to him, I did not want him or need him. I was terrified of what might happen if I got his attention as I knew how I felt around a guy I liked, and it was a lot easier to not have to experience that excruciating awkwardness if I got too close.

However, I honestly believed a "celebrity" would never be interested in me. I was safe. We were a far distance apart. When I felt ready, I was going to flash a smile with eye contact at the super handsome man that made my insides shine in delight. Well, that was my natural state, but my mind sometimes attached it to him making me feel like that.

I still wasn't expecting any other interactions. He was a celebrity, who was I? No one! That is what I believed at that time anyway. I felt amazing and wonderful. I enjoyed the rest of the event, dancing and chatting with new people, and making new Facebook friends.

I even got up on the stage to dance! I had an amazing time until I thought "shit! What am I doing up here? How do I get off the stage without anyone looking at me? I managed to leave the stage and then I went to the toilet, hoping by the time I went back I would have been forgotten about by everyone watching me.

I looked innocent and tried to blend back in with the people I was with. When I looked up at the handsome guy, he had his head down, and looked like he was squirming a bit with a little smirk. Like "uh oh! Why did she do that?!"

I pretended not to see and stood playing dumb and unaware. Then I glanced over in the direction of the main head female celebrity in charge of it all, glaring right at me with a deep evil glare.

"Oh!" I winced in pain! I hated doing things wrong and upsetting people. I didn't like making people hate me. I pretended I didn't care though and looked the other way. I frazzled the discomfort, and she was eradicated from my consciousness.

I was never going to allow the way another person looked at me to make me feel bad. If someone looks at me badly because of a mistake I made, let them.

She oversaw the whole event. If I, someone that often felt inadequate could cause such a stir to a woman in charge, then I must be pretty powerful myself! I let it make me feel good.

Eventually, the attention was off me, and everyone was enjoying the event. At one point, the ultra-sexy man took his top off and had his fun moment on the stage.

I missed it as I was sitting around the other side, which I was glad about because it would have made me cringe and I didn't want to have any negative judgements against him. I wanted to have good feelings towards him. All though looking back it would have been better to not have him on such a pedestal. Once the event had finished, I decided to make a quick exit to get myself home. By some fluke, I passed the painfully attractive man, and he held out his hand to me. I was so shocked with delight and amazement; all I could do was stare at it. Fear that I might do something wrong by shaking his hand.

"OMG!" I eventually shook his hand, crumbling on the inside. To me, he was this amazing human being!! I couldn't believe it; I couldn't believe he wanted to interact with me in the flesh. To top it off he told me to add him on Instagram. At that moment I could not remember his name if I had ever known it.

My ego liked not knowing the name of a so-called "celebrity"; it meant I could force myself to not see him as above me; on a soul level I know we are all equal anyway.

I felt like I was the naughtiest girl in the world, blushing deeply on the inside to have caught the attention of what I thought was one of the sexiest men ever!

I was partly super excited and squealing more than ever internally, mostly from immense fear of things going wrong, but I was also super cool on the outside, because you must keep cool right?

Looking back, it would have been better to act overly excited and needy and have turned him off me.

I told him, "I will find you!" I felt so naughty, I felt bad, all these sexual feelings going on inside of me, going wild with joy.

I was unaware that I had gone back to my old ways. I knew the tools, correct? I knew psychology, I would be fine.

All the feelings I felt were too much for me to handle and they made me feel excruciatingly embarrassed at the thought of anyone finding out.

I managed to find his Instagram account when I went home, "Rose's Jack", and I was amazed to see he had tens of thousands of followers. I couldn't believe it. I was in total awe of him! He was like a massive celebrity.

"Insta famous" my sister called him. I had never heard of "Rose's Jack" before, but all his photos made me gush and melt. I loved looking at him. I had never experienced that before.

His Instagram account not only had (what I believed at the time to be) gorgeous photos of himself but the words that matched the photographs connected to my heart and soul and made me gush even more.

I was taken a back with so much awe when I saw that he had reverted to become a Muslim. I had started to learn about the religion Islam and thought about becoming a Muslim myself. I always felt a bit silly doing it though and I could never fully follow through with it. I was going to church, and I felt bad leaving them behind.

When I saw his post about being celibate and waiting for the one woman to be with and marry; I wanted him badly. I wanted him so badly, but I knew that what I was feeling was not in control. I knew how I felt couldn't be real love. Even so, in my eyes at that time, he was my perfect man and I wanted to get close to him!

When I saw he even spoke about "finding his twin soul," I couldn't believe he even knew about this deep spiritual concept.

I knew of it as the "twin flame." He was the one, I was adamant he was it! I didn't think many people know about the "twin flame." He had to be the one!

I did not believe that I could ever feel like I did, and it wasn't my one and only meant to be with twin flame. I was in total awe.

We should never be in awe unless in the presence of the creator. We must only ever feel deep gratitude and appreciation to the creator.

I thought the drop dead gorgeous man would have forgotten me by the time he got home. I thought he would have missed my follow notification and I would never ever hear from him.

When I saw that he requested to follow my private Instagram account, I felt knocked back. Swept off my feet already. I had to calm myself down. I had completely forgotten about feeling carefree and not caring about him and not needing him.

I had forgotten the energy I gave off to attract him in the first place. The energy of total happiness without him. I was trembling and weak at the knees. I had to take deep breaths to keep cool. I had to remind myself that "so what! All he did was follow my page! That doesn't mean anything!"

Sex: Good or Bad?

Once upon a time if I felt that way about a man, I may have sent them a boring "hi, how are you?" message to see if they responded. Desperate for any kind of interaction.

Once upon a time I may have even sent a dirty sex talk message to capture their attention, but I had come a long way since then. I knew I wasn't going to have sex with this man unless we were married. His Instagram page clearly stated it.

I accepted his follow request and eagerly hoped he would message me. I certainly wasn't going to message him first. It wasn't to play cool either, it was to give myself time to calm down and forget him, focus my attention on more important things. Make sure I wasn't going to lose my mind over him. Pine for him. Get myself back to being me. I did not think he would ever message me.

When I saw that he had messaged me, I screamed out loud in delight. I was ecstatic and over the moon. I grinned from ear to ear and started taking in lots of deep breaths again.

At least I could express my feelings, as I was not physically in his presence. I couldn't "scare" him away because I was hiding behind a screen and my Instagram account photos.

I was still mortified about the way I felt though. It was so degrading!

Even though I had been taught by Rori Raye to communicate all my real authentic feelings and be open and share them, I guess I didn't feel safe doing so. I felt I needed him that much! I felt stupid and silly because I had never even sat down and had a conversation with him. I guess what I felt was intense infatuation.

I cannot stress enough! Feel your deep crazy feelings when they arise. If it is too much, you will have gotten your feelings out there and then to be frazzled and not bottled up for the mind to start chattering away at you.

It is much more important to release feelings exactly when they arise, if the other gets scared off, good! Scare them away!

You're not ready for such a man or woman, either that OR you will be escaping a dangerous situation.

I can't remember the conversation we had but he ended up giving me his number. I couldn't believe it. I suddenly felt like a naughty little girl with a secret. But a naughty little secret I was happy with, not being told to keep it a secret with deep shame, even though my feelings did make me feel ashamed.

How I felt was too much and I didn't want anyone to know about it. Not even him. He gave me his phone number and I had to remind myself it didn't mean anything. I sent him a text message so he had my number, and he could message or call me if he wanted to.

We had a few phone calls and video calls and I had resorted to my painfully shy, shut down mode, barely able to say anything but I didn't completely shut off my feelings, I allowed my shy coyness to come out. Blushing a bit. I had all these sexual feelings towards him, and I felt like how I felt in the past after having sex with a man I was never keen on and some pushed themselves onto me, I felt like that with him, and we hadn't even had sex.

On one of those video calls, I told him that I too was celibate like him. I told him I went to church, and I was waiting for marriage. He then suggested we get married.

I smiled and nodded, and I felt so excited inside. I was going to get married and be able have sex without any shame. Sex without being abandoned and sex that was right in the eyes of God. I couldn't wait to feel safe to feel my real emotions. I had to really see it and believe it before opening myself up properly to him. I had to stay vigilant incase this was too good to be true.

Huge mistake I made trying to stay in control, and not feel my emotions. All though perhaps it wasn't!

The huge mistake was believing what this man said to me and believing his Instagram posts before ever properly having the chance to meet him in person.

Sex: Good or Bad?

I never wanted to message or call him first because I didn't want to "chase him" and scare him off. I believed my intense emotions would have scared him away, but I kept wondering when I would get a call or a message from him, and I couldn't wait for that moment.

The reality was, if I scared him away then good, but in my experience, men just melt in awe and look like they get shivers.

My fear was bigger than being able to feel my emotions. The people that do get scared away from you feeling your deep in-depth feelings, are the kind of people that don't like losing control. They must be in control. These people don't know true freedom.

Often, we're not actually feeling our true authentic feelings, we're covering it up with something dramatic that is because of fear.

I was sure I would be in his presence one day so I could use all the tools I had learnt from Rori and be able to slip in various psychology phrases at suitable moments. It was about 1 month from the time of the event and to the time I eventually had an invite to see him.

He called me not long after my mum told me my cousin had died and I felt a lot of pain. I was crying and in distress. He sounded worried about me. He told me he had a friend there and we would go out and drive around in the car. I didn't really like the sound of a friend being there, but I said "OK". If I got to be near him, it didn't matter.

I felt sad about my cousin but the happy, satisfied feeling of finally getting to be with this beautiful man, the man that I believed was my twin flame, took my mind off it which I was so grateful for and relieved. I had dropped my son off to his dads for the weekend and I was free the whole weekend. I couldn't wait to have the company of my twin flame soul, the man that said we were going to marry.

I didn't tell anyone because I knew how crazy it would have

sounded to others. I wanted to see it myself and then let everyone see it for themselves. I had forgotten to tell anyone that I was going to meet the handsome man that was a stranger and stay at his place.

Luckily though while I was on the train towards London, my dear friend Jeff messaged me, and I suddenly realised that it would be a good idea to keep safe, just in case, to tell someone where I was going.

It is interesting because I don't often hear from Jeff, there are long periods of time between each interaction but even so, I love him dearly. Looking back, I am so glad he messaged me so I could let him know of my whereabouts.

Rose's Jack even asked me while I was there, "Did you tell anyone where you were going?"

I told him about Jeff, he then said, "Clever!".

When I got to London I then got onto the relevant tube to the relevant stop where I planned to meet the gorgeous heart throb of a male. My belly went all giddy when we were finally together, I took a deep breath to compose myself. I couldn't believe this was happening. I was in the presence of a famous Instagram celeb that I thought looked like a super model in his pictures. I was thrilled.

I couldn't wait to see the apartment where he lived in central London to get cosy and warm. I was shocked when I saw he lived in a council flat. It wasn't just any council flat; it was a bit grimy in places and it didn't even have any carpet.

It made me feel strange and something immediately felt off, however, I wasn't going to judge him or take my presence away from him because of his apartment. The thought of that made me feel guilty. I was not a shallow person. I was going to be the most loving, loyal, and faithful partner he had ever had. I would find out later that I wouldn't be getting that back from him though.

Why? I wasn't being loyal, faithful, and loving to myself. I wasn't committed to taking care of myself. I wasn't allowing my real feelings to be expressed.

I couldn't believe I was in his presence and the smell of delicious food cooking and him telling me he had cooked it, distracted me from any doubts I had about this man. He dished me up some food onto a plate and it was delicious. I hadn't had a home cooked meal for a while. I almost picked up the plate and licked it, but that would have been extremely bad mannered, so I refrained from doing so. He must have seen what I was about to do, and then eagerly he said,

"Yes, go on, lick the plate!" He looked very keen to see me perform what my mother would have called "disgusting". I thought about it for a second. I did like the taste of this but then I felt embarrassed at the thought of being so impolite.

I blushed and said "no" in my most polite manner. He came and sat next to me. "You can if you want to." I smiled coyly and shook my head to say "no" again. Looking back, I am sure he had a food fetish.

We took a walk to the shop, and he bought a kettle so I could drink tea. I felt very looked after by him. It was a wonderful feeling, but I was still painfully shy and found feeling and speaking immensely difficult around him.

I should have said, "I am so grateful for you doing this for me. I am getting a warm loving feeling from it" and felt the feeling as I said it. I wasn't confident at all around him.

He bought a movie for us to watch and lots of sweets, chocolate, crisps, and ice cream to have while watching it.

Even though he was a Muslim man and didn't drink alcohol at all, he offered to buy me alcohol while in the alcohol section. However, much of it would have made me feel more relaxed. I mostly wanted to do right by God myself and I said no. I really wanted to be a good Muslim like he was, and I really wanted to get married to him. Then we could have sex. Something at that time I would have loved to have felt safe and happy about doing.

I just blushed and smiled most of the time. The crazy strong feelings I felt made me shut down. Later that night while we were in bed together, we were kissing and cuddling, and I felt uncomfortable because we weren't married yet. I was sure he wasn't going to try it on with me, all the way.

However, his hands were lustfully feeling my all over the bare skin on my back and body and just as he was about to go into my knickers. I totally surrendered to God. The deepest part of my soul, I was there because I believed he was celibate and wanted to wait for marriage. I believed I was safe with this holy man.

I knew I had done no wrong in my heart, I was believing God and doing my best to follow the right path. I hadn't even had a glass of wine.

My heart was totally open to this man because I believed he knew God like I did. I believed he was like me, felt bad for all his past shame and became Muslim and wanted to make things right with God.

I felt safe totally surrendering to God, God had always saved me when I was able to go deep like that before. I didn't know I would be saved, but when feeling afraid that is where I automatically go to.

I managed to release the word, "no" in the sweetest, most vulnerable voice. I was afraid and I felt safe to feel it because I knew God, I was there because of my trust in God and knowing I wanted to do the right thing.

I had been in that situation so many times before, but I had rarely been listened to or respected. I didn't try to sound sweet and vulnerable; it was genuine from my soul connecting to God. I was about to cry to and from God in the purest way if he didn't stop.

Yes, he was sexy. Yes, he was fit and yes, I would have loved to have let my sex addiction part of me loose. Allow him into me and become close, become one and deeply intimate… but I needed to know I was safe doing so with God on my side.

I knew if I did that, it wasn't going to be good for being close to God. God was more important to me than anything. God made me feel safe. God always saved me in moments of terror. I needed to feel safe.

Before when I had said "no" and not been listened to, I never allowed the truth of my fear to show. It was a meek, "no" hoping they would listen. Or at times it was a whiney "no."

Sometimes I might have giggled and said "no." For some reason whenever I said "no" before I felt like I was to blame. I was there alone with the guy and had never discussed what I wanted and what I expected of him. I was also very shy.

I guess if I was to blame, it would have been from not being able to feel my truest deepest feelings from the soul.

I couldn't believe it when Jack whipped himself away from me quickly and had a look of shame on his face. It was so beautiful, and I felt so safe. He put his arm around me, and I lay my head on his chest while we cuddled. I loved being in this man's presence more than anything.

I concluded that he wasn't celibate at all. I realised he likely had a lot of women on the go. I then believed that he probably wanted to be good by God, but all the women just swooned over him, and he wasn't able to stop himself as he was a man with his male instincts. It was up to the women not to allow him. I was not going to allow him.

CHAPTER 23

Twin Flame Hell Part 2

The next evening, Rose's Jack called up the head female celebrity from the event. He had the call on loudspeaker. She sounded vulnerable.

He asked her, "What's the matter, are you ok?"

She replied, "I love you."

My immediate response came from my heart. "Awwwhhh" I said gently. I also wanted her to know I was his woman; I was with him, and we were together.

I thought to myself, of course, she loves him. Who wouldn't? I believed he was a super sexy Godly man. I didn't feel jealous because I knew Muslim men could have 4 wives. I was going to be his wife and I guessed that she had already slept with him, which meant she had already failed, that was my belief at that time anyway.

At some point later in the evening, Jack asked me a question which I had already answered. "Where are you from?"

I replied in confusion, "I was born in Brighton, but I don't remember it as I was a baby, I moved to Eastbourne, then..."

"No. No. No. What intelligence agency are you from?" He jumped up and stood in front of me to see all my reactions."

In shock and confusion, I replied, "Why would I be from an

intelligence agency?" He then quickly said, "I don't know, there is nothing going on around here!"

I then looked around, feeling very uneasy.

He quickly responded again in his hyperactive manner and love-bombing state, "I don't know, it's just you're so intelligent."

I blushed and swooned over the positive attention. No one had ever described me as intelligent before. It was a huge compliment to me. My heart expanded even more. He then quickly said, "Come on, let's go and get some food!" He grabbed my hand and pulled me into the kitchen before I could think anymore, about what he had just said.

I stayed another night and on Sunday morning we played around in the bedroom. I whined in frustration, "Oh... we need to get married right now!!" He looked taken aback.

Suddenly he agreed. "You're right, we need to get married right now!" He whisked me into the other room where two of his friends were and said, "We need to get married right now! Please can you marry us!"

One of his friends grinned and the other one looked a bit ashamed. Then he suddenly said some words, we said some words that could have been described as vows if it had been a proper wedding, and we both said, "I do."

Then he whisked me back into the bedroom and tried it on with me again. He said, "we're married now!"

I said, "That wasn't real!"

"Then why did you go along with it?"

"Because it's fun" I screeched with giggles and laughter. Feeling more confident to feel my feelings.

He suddenly turned serious, "Oh my God! I really really really like you!"

I felt so taken care of by such a strong man, or so I thought. I went home to be with my son and get him to school the next day and to send him off for his school trip for the week.

Jack messaged me and asked me to go back straight away. I needed to be in London and up early for a film shoot so I was incredibly happy to stay again with a good excuse, so it didn't look like I was only there for him.

My son was away all week, so it was perfect but also, I was desperate to be as close to Rose's Jack as I possibly could be, always. I felt safe. I believed he was my twin soul.

He really liked that I was an actress, and I spent the next few days at his flat with him. He went away to work every morning and I was happy to wait for him. I was still super nervous and not 100% comfortable but it was better than being home on my own.

One day he came back from work and said to only his friend, "Oh my God! Is she still here!" He told me I could stay the week, so I felt very hurt and confused.

Anyone with self-respect would have gotten up and just left there and then, not me. I wanted to stay with my sweetheart, my twin flame. I also felt in a bit of survival mode, frozen survival mode.

On another evening he told me he had a friend coming around. He told me to pretend I was just a flatmate. I said it was OK. It turned out to be one of the other Z list celebrities from the event, another female. I was shocked, but of course, I was very polite and friendly towards her.

While we were all in the kitchen he pointed at her fluffy cream jumper, "is that new?" He asked her. She said it was. I just thought it was normal for her to have a new jumper but now I am thinking she specifically went out to get herself a new jumper to spend the evening with him in.

I then knew I had competition, but I was not afraid. I still believed if I didn't have sex with him, I would win him over with all the tools I learnt.

At any given moment when I was able to feel deeply, I did... I touched her jumper and let my whole body react in a way that showed I enjoyed the softness and said, "ooo, it is so soft!"

He looked at me. I was happy. I had his attention.

A bit later, we were all sitting on the bed. She was in the middle of us. I longed to be next to him, but I didn't care too much, I was still in the same room as him.

He started kissing her and I noticed that he was looking at me to see my reaction. I just thought, "do what you like! I don't care, as long as I can be with you too. Muslims can have four wives and I am happy if you care for me like a man."

I loved him. I adored him and nothing was to stop that feeling I had for him. Even though his actions were clearly showing me he was not the man he made out to be on Instagram, I couldn't change my mind or my feelings. I was adamant that I could make him be the man he made out to be on Instagram. I refused to believe he was a complete fake and a complete fraud.

"Perhaps he tried to be the man on Instagram, but it was too hard with all the girls easily having sex with him whenever he wanted it." I came up with all kinds of excuses for him.

I really believed if I didn't have sex with him easily, I could make him want me. I had to. I was shut off from the truth because I was so desperate! Cringe!

I remember just staring at her. I knew if I just stared at her it would make her feel uncomfortable and hopefully, she would soon leave. It worked and I was relieved to have him all to myself again.

After she left Rose's Jack got a bit physical with me again, lifting up my top to reveal my breasts. I thought "Ok, let's just do this now!"

We didn't. He left me hanging and feeling confused.

Rose's Jack knew I was leaving the next morning, but he said he wasn't going to say goodbye as if I was leaving. I found it a bit strange and a bit hurtful, but I was also relieved to be going home and having my son return from his school trip. It had been a crazy roller coaster of a week. I believed that I had enjoyed my week off and spending it with Roses' Jack. The reality was, it was all subtly very abusive which I refused to acknowledge.

When I got home, I messaged Roses' Jack to let him know I arrived home safely like he asked me to do. I told him I felt better, and the foggy cloud had been lifted. I told him because in my warped mind he cared about me, and those were my true feelings.

The first thing he replied to me was "come back." It made my heart beam with joy. I was so happy. I would have loved to have gone back but obviously I couldn't have as I had my gorgeous perfect son to care for. My life saver!

Also, I knew it was good to leave some distance between us. I still believed that because I didn't have sex with him, I still had some kind of chance with him.

The fact that he lied on his Instagram, and I trusted him with the marriage thing is what made me ruin the number one rule that must always be stuck to. NEVER go to a guy's house on the first date and especially NOT to sleep over and NEVER let a man into your own house on or after a first date either.

The first date is ALWAYS out in public somewhere. Whether he is trustworthy or not, you won't know, and he knows you won't know. He needs to be tested.

I thought because my friend at the time knew him, I believed he was already an acquaintance and I thought he was OK. It was not OK. My "so called" friend hardly knew him either.

The fact that his whole Instagram was fake and fraudulent, meant he was an extremely dangerous person to meet in real life. Unfortunately, I had fallen for his lies, and it was all too late. My weakness of men but my strength for God was a bad but also incredible combination. The incredible part is the learning experience I got from it to be able to share with you.

I couldn't stop thinking about him and when he would next call me and want to meet up.

I had just spent a whole week with him, of course he would call me to meet up. I was adamant that I wasn't going to call or message him. I would wait for as long as I needed to. Even though we hadn't had sex I still felt the deep desperate feelings for him as if we had had sex. I was in a fantasy relationship with him that he had encouraged.

When I hadn't heard from him for about 2 or 3 weeks my angry revenge started to kick in.

The part of me that felt deep pain because I had opened my heart up to him deeply in love. He hadn't used me for sex though, but he had tried. My heart was wide open to him because of my belief that he was a Godly and good man.

The angry revenge part is when I think I am getting something from a man, but it isn't followed through with. If I had sex with a guy, not always but when I felt the revenge feeling, I would expect love and a committed relationship, and they were just using me.

Or if I was confident that someone had done wrong to me, by not accepting my "no", if I felt safe and confident in myself, I would want to get revenge on them. "How dare they!"

With Jacks, I expected love and marriage, and I hadn't even met him properly or interacted with him in person. He did say that we would marry but knowing that people can lie, I should have seen it for myself.

He spoke to my ego and told me he had never been with a blond-haired woman before. My ego thought my looks were enough to secure him. My head had constantly been ticking over about the week I was there and everything I had witnessed and the fact he had so many other women on the go, and he wasn't even married to any of them.

Looking back, I should have thought that if he had never been with a blond-haired woman before then perhaps, he wouldn't have been attracted to them. I was blinded!

If he had called me and given me the attention that I desperately craved, then I wouldn't have kept going into the dark part of pain that made me think I wanted revenge.

Even if that was true, that is blaming him for my feelings and reactions, but the truth is I should have kept present and been in each moment I was in. Out of my head, not in my mind. Not thinking about him. Not letting him warp my brain. Men are free to do what they want but lying and manipulating is cruel. Even so, we still must take responsibility for our own selves.

I kept thinking about him. I couldn't stop it. I suddenly realised that his name was not Roses' Jack. I suddenly realised that in one of the most Romantic films I had ever seen, "Titanic" the lead characters' names were Rose and Jack. I was gobsmacked.

I knew a bit about psychology and people's brains; had he given himself the name on purpose to make women desperately fall for him? I couldn't believe it. I thought I wouldn't let him know right away that I knew but when he eventually got in touch, I would share it.

However, he still hadn't contacted me. I believed I was in love and in pain. Rejected. I had a lot of unprocessed pain that came to the surface.

My evil revenge kicked in and I ended up messaging the head female of the event, the one that told Jack "I love you."

I messaged her and told her everything, everything about when I stayed the week. HE tried it on with me, he kissed the other woman in front of me, and I told her about another lady I found that was his main woman, after doing some research on him. I even mentioned that his name wasn't even Roses' Jack!

Sex: Good or Bad?

I knew she would confront him about it. I also wanted him to know I knew his secret. I wanted his attention. To me he was my twin flame. Meant to be from God and we were supposed to be happy together. Absolutely barking mad!

I knew my action would make him angry and exposed and I was extremely nervous about when he would call me to confront me; I was also excited to hear from him again. I just wanted his attention. I wanted to hear his voice. I wanted him to remember me, I wanted to be important to him. I felt nervous, excited, and relieved I had shared my built-up thoughts with another, and proud of myself too for a few hours. I felt strong. It was of course for my ego that was experiencing extreme pain.

I can't say that he was all to blame, even though he lied, and I trusted him.

It is very silly to put all your trust, blindly and openly in someone you have only just met, as Adam Mussa has also taught me. Unfortunately, that is what abuse survivors often do.

Opening yourself up so deeply, just because their internet profile claims that they know God and are devoted to their religion. The way that I felt about him I didn't think I would ever feel about anyone ever again. If I had sex with someone, then I was closed off from my emotions and I chose to not feel attached. Exactly how a prostitute has sex.

I didn't think any man could get me to feel anything so deeply ever again.

Eventually my phone started ringing and the name read that it was him. My heart leapt a beat in excitement and also complete fear.

I bravely answered it to hear what he was going to say. I was still incredibly quiet and shy with him and embarrassed. He didn't scream, shout or yell but I could tell he wasn't happy with me. I felt high from what I had done and a high from speaking with him. I felt happy. I had gotten everything off my chest. He knew I wasn't a woman to mess with.

I would learn that he wasn't a man to mess with either!

It wasn't long though until I started thinking good thoughts about him again and pining for him, desperately feeling like I needed him. I started chatting regularly to his ex, his once was main woman.

She told me lots and lots of things about him. Secrets that shouldn't have been told. The stuff he did that was extremely fraudulent. She also told me that the day I went there they had an argument and the dinner I ate believing Jack cooked it, she had made it. Hearing the truth felt incredible! I thanked her and told her it was delicious.

I was amazed at everything I heard! She let me know he paid for his Instagram followers, and they weren't real. He paid for all the likes on his photos. It was the first I had ever heard of it. Paying to have a huge following.

I read a bit about it, and I learnt that if someone has lots of followers and not many comments on their thread, then the followers are fake. Real famous Instagrammers have many comments to match their likes and followers.

His ex-told me that even a close-up picture of a six-pack abs didn't belong to him and was a photo from the internet of somebody else. I couldn't believe how much fakery someone would go into just to look better than they were and to fool others.This was all fascinating news and gossip for my ego to revel in.

I still pined for him though and I still believed I loved him, an infatuation I could not stop. I felt sorry for him, and it made my love deepen for him even more. To be such a liar he must be in pain and not believe in his true magnificent power that I knew and still know exists in him and in all of us.

I had read so many times that a man will never change, but I didn't need him to change, I needed him to accept my love. Love he did not want to receive. Fake love. Infatuation.True, real love, the love is reciprocated. True real love wants the other to be happy and free and knowing they already have enough love where they are, or they have the freedom not to accept and experience love.

I did not feel I had any love where I was. Even though I want-ed him to be happy and free, I wanted something from him, even if it was just his presence that I believed to be great. I couldn't let him be and I couldn't feel at peace without him. He invaded my thoughts and I just wanted to be near him, to feel the feeling of love I believed he had the power over me to make me feel.

False love wants to possess. Even though I didn't want to possess him, I certainly seemed to have been possessed by him!

False love hurts like crazy. False love is a projection of past pain and is needed to come up to be processed and acknowledged so it can be released.

My body wanted to have sex with him, animalistic; but my soul wanted marriage. My mind was a complete mess. When I knew marriage wasn't on the cards, I made the physical body sensations believe it was love.

But it wasn't love. Love is soft, kind, and gentle. Love grows when you give and receive moments of presence that are positive for each other and trustworthy.

I was happy to hear that his ex was adamant that she was incredibly happy with someone else and would never ever go back to him ever again. It was a huge relief to know that there was one less woman chasing him. The woman that said she was his main woman, and he always went back to her, and her to him.

Because of my mind going crazy, constantly thinking about him and not being able to get him out of my head, it felt good chat-ting to someone about him that knew him. It was fun when she would call me up to tell me gossip about anything she heard.

Even though I knew it was wrong to gossip, hearing anything

at all felt so good. I was in a very dark place.

The pain was still agonising, and I didn't know what to do. I started journaling and writing all my feelings down, to make sure I didn't contact him. I poured out my deepest feelings, every day I would sit and write something from the depth of my core, hoping one day soon he would contact me without me having to contact him first.

About 3 months passed by and still I hadn't heard anything from him. It was so painful, yet I was too embarrassed to contact him. Men always eventually contacted me! I just had to wait! I was on a completely different energy level to when I first attracted him, I was desperate.

I came across an article by the lovely relationship coach Renee Wade, the Feminine woman. The article said the "leaning back" approach won't always work because a guy may be interested but he doesn't think you're interested. It made so much sense to me.

A high-value woman can do as she pleases because she doesn't depend on the man for her happiness. The problem was I had not been acting in a high-value state of being, and I certainly wasn't at the time of reading the article. The way I felt was needy and desperate.

Rori does mention in her work that if you're in a high value place of course you can reach out to a man. If not, then he will sense it. When you're in a high value place, you're never dependent on an interaction with a man to make you happy.

The way I felt, I wasn't happy in my own skin on my own. At the time my happiness depended on him. I believed I needed him to make me happy and feel good. I was a mess!

I ended up sending him all the pages I had written via email. Did he reply? I don't remember but if he did it wasn't enough.

I felt frustrated that sharing my deep written feelings hadn't worked, so I messaged a model that I knew, knew him, Bethany

Sex: Good or Bad?

Rose. It was not a good message about him.

I knew that talking badly about him to another would make him contact me. He did.

Obviously, I did not get a good reaction from him, and I felt guilty for not being loving towards him. The pain and desperation of needing to be with him was too much. I needed an excuse to go to London so I could casually pop by.

Feeling terrified, I messaged Sara, my old school friend that had moved to London. We always had fun together. I knew she would at least take my mind off him for a while if I was too afraid to go through with it.

I met her on Friday and the next evening was Saturday. She was visiting a friend relatively nearby Rose's Jack or whatever his name was; so, she was happy to come with me!

We had a few glasses of wine at her house before we left to go to Jack's. Then we went to the pub near his apartment to have an extra drink for Dutch courage before making our way over. I knew he was a very dodgy character and there was a chance he was extremely dangerous. One last thing I thought before going to his apartment was,

"What if he kills me?" I decided to update my Facebook status, just in-case anything happened.

"I forgot to buy a lottery ticket for tonight, but I am about to take a huge gamble right now!" It made me feel safer, just in case. I had bought Jack some chocolates from hotel Chocolat, and I added some love notes in with the bag too, sharing pieces of my heart.

I knew everything I was doing was completely wrong and against everything I had learnt from Rori Raye, but I felt desperate, and I still believed he was my twin flame. It felt better to express myself this time when I saw him, than hold everything in, even if it was against all the advice.

My plan was to express my true feelings in-front of him. If he could see me in person, feeling everything fully, it might work. I had nothing to lose, apart from my life, but at least then the pain I felt would end with it.

My darling friend, Sara, came with me to the front door of his flat. Suddenly, I wasn't sure what I was going to do. Suddenly, the fear choked a hold of me. I was shaking with nerves a bit too. I had suddenly chickened out and I didn't know what I was going to say to him. I decided I would knock on the door, give him the present and then quickly leave.

Sex: Good or Bad?

CHAPTER 24

Twin Flame Hell part 3

bravely knocked loudly, a few times. I knew a quiet knock would leave me standing outside wondering if he had heard it or not and if I should knock again.

I heard his voice. "Who is it?" I felt sick. I couldn't believe I was doing it in real life. There was no way I could have done it without my friend by my side.

"Delivery" My quick thinking called back. I decided to turn my back to the spy hole and hold up the delivery. I heard him come close to the door.

He gradually opened the door and I felt myself gasp as I caught a glimpse of him through the ajar. He opened the door a bit more and I jiggled the bag of chocolates and love notes, and gently thrust them closer to him, to take.

Instead of taking the bag, he then opened the door even wider and made a small gesture to summon me in, still partly hiding behind the door. I was in awe!

Really?! Was he going to let me inside... again? My insides danced with love and joy. I was still extremely nervous as I still had no idea how this evening was going to pan out. I took a deep breath and stepped inside. I was falsely standing with huge confidence. I had to or I would have felt like a small mouse again, like when I stayed with him before. I needed to feel big and confident, like I did not care! I followed him to his bedroom and when I stepped inside there was a man I had not met before sitting on the sofa.

Sara came into the bedroom too. She sat on the bed and Jack sat on the sofa next to his friend. I didn't feel it was polite to sit down uninvited, so I stayed standing. I stood feeling extremely uncomfortable but refusing to feel my real feelings; what I had planned to do, my whole reasoning for being there. I forced myself to look strong and confident, knowing what he did was wrong. Looking back, I must have looked a bit threatening.

When I noticed his hand go slowly down beside him in a very controlled focussed manner, I looked down at it and then back at him to say, "what is that?" He then pointed at the bed as if I should sit on it. I suddenly felt shy and embarrassed.

"Really? You want me to sit down here?" I thought as I blushed.

Rose's Jack then made another gesture with his hand and nodded his head. Not only was I now inside his flat again, but he wanted me to sit down on his bed again too. WOW!

I enjoyed the present moment of the gift he was giving me by sitting on his bed. I welcomed it and felt the feeling of being at home. I felt a wave of calmness. I felt relaxed for the first time in an exceptionally long time.

I enjoyed the feeling of love and let it flow through me.

"What are you doing here?" He spoke.

I suddenly felt awkward and out of place and played dumb. "I'm not sure. What are we doing here Sara?" I asked.

She suddenly started to say the reason why and I started to feel immensely embarrassed, and I did not want to disclose my deep feelings after all.

Instead of staying quiet and shy, I let myself express myself, even if it was not normal. I did not care. It was better to be a million percent myself and abnormal than hold in my true self and hide the awkward explosive feelings that were to cover up the intimate feelings that I knew were crazy!

I quickly talked over her in a hyper manner. "No no no no no no, don't say it! Shhhhh!" I said, flapping my hands around. I couldn't bear to hear what she was going to say, and I didn't want to be looked at.

"No, no, no, no!" I squeezed my eyes shut and put my hands over my ears. "La, la, la, la, la, I am not listening!" I wailed as I threw myself back on the bed. I continued with a few more "la la's" pretending no one else was around me; until I decided to be quiet, to hear if she had stopped explaining the reason why we were there.To my relief, no one was talking. I still made sure I continued to zone everyone out. I opened my eyes and looked over at a little table. It had a lightning globe on it. I put my focus and attention onto it. I had to get myself back to a normal state. I needed to feel calm.

When I felt relaxed and calm, I managed to look over at the others. Silent. Jack was staring at me shocked, with a slight smile of disbelief on his face. "What was that?"

All that mattered was that I was able to keep calm. My little outburst was over. I sat back on the edge of the bed, feeling very silly and embarrassed. I didn't know who was going to speak next or what they were going to say.

I looked at another little table. There was a miniature toy looking gun covered in dazzling crystals. The sparkling beauty of it had me mesmerised and I couldn't stop staring at it for ages, but I felt afraid to express my excitement because it was a gun, violent, but the sparkles made me feel calm. I couldn't take my eyes off it!

I remembered a conversation we had had when I stayed the week a few months back. I remembered he had said that in America everyone has a gun and then his eyes looked towards his chest of drawers.

When I looked where he looked and thought "no! He doesn't have a gun! Does he?" I couldn't believe a holy religious man would have a gun in his apartment. "We're supposed to be good and not have violent weapons around".

His eyes widened, "Come on, let's go get some food." Then he quickly dragged me into the kitchen to take my attention away from my thoughts.

During my crazy thinking time I was going to love him anyhow, whoever he was and whatever he had done. I wanted to keep all his secrets like a very loyal person.

I was desperate to show my feelings of excitement and happiness at the pretty crystals. It was bursting inside me, but the gun part made me feel afraid to do so.

I decided to pick something else up off the table to express my bursting feelings of joy.

"Ooooo, what is this?" I said in pure excitement and ecstasy. When I took a closer look at it, it was a piece of cheese. I was mortified that it looked like I had just expressed those feelings over a piece of cheese.

"It's cheeeeeeese!" I said, in disappointment and not being able to hide my horror, because I was here to express all my feelings! The cheese wasn't something I could get away with being excited over and the thought of him looking at me getting excited over the cheese was rather humiliating!

I have often giggled about that to this day! I put the cheese back on the table as if to say, "Well, that can just stay there then!" I glanced over at Jack, and he was really smirking and looking highly entertained.

I thought, "Yeah! That is good. He is smiling!" I felt calm again and just sat on the edge of the bed, getting myself into a new moment and dissolving the last few embarrassing moments.

More conversations occurred.

At one point Sara started sticking up for Jack and I just lost my temper and I shouted at her. She ended up storming out of the flat.

Jack asked if I was going to go after her. I wanted to but I felt more afraid being away from my twin flame.

I shook my head and explained with sadness that she was going to meet a man that she was giving blowjobs. A man that was obviously using her and it made me feel sad, but I knew she would just go and do as she pleases anyway.

It was just me, Jack, and his friend. I felt uncomfortable and extremely awkward, so I decided to sit on my hands to distract myself and try to get more comfortable.

Jack suddenly approached me and told me to stand up and turn around. He searched me all over, then told me to bend over and searched me some more. I was submissive to everything Jack said. I surrendered to my core; my mind terrified but knowing underneath the true feelings got released in the moment.

When I was bent over with sexy Jack standing behind me, I felt the height of sexiness. I slowly turned around, taking a deep breath with my lips slightly parted, and gave him eyes to say, "come on then" and one of my eyebrows twitched alongside it.

I wanted to have sex with him. While I was away from him, I regretted not having sex with him. I wished that if I had just been my promiscuous sex addicted self, and satisfied myself sexually with him, then I would have heard back from him eventually. Either that or I wouldn't have heard back from him at all, but it might have felt easier.

Of course, his first reaction was to just stare back into my eyes, and I am fairly sure for a few seconds he looked a bit vulnerable. He took a deep breath, then glanced at his friend on the sofa, then quickly back at me, then he backed off and away back to sit next to his friend.

His friend said something that I didn't hear but then Jack quickly responded, "No way! No way, I am not giving myself to her! Not after what she did!"

Sex: Good or Bad?

I felt deep sadness and I wasn't afraid to let it show through my eyes from my soul and on my face, in hope my true feelings would bring him close. It didn't, but it was sure as heaven an amazing release. It felt wonderful.

I still don't remember the exact exchange of words after that, but do I remember in pure anger and pure hatred and pure evilness, screaming at him from the pit of my being where I had been hurt repeatedly, again and again, by many different men,

"Because I hate men and that's yoooooooooooou!" I didn't know narcissists or sociopaths had any feelings or emotions, but for one or two seconds, our inner essences were connected through the eyes. I saw sadness there. While I didn't feel anything at that moment as I was too caught up in my own pain and I was expressing it. I felt powerful.

When I looked back at this moment for the whole time that I still pinned and yearned for him, loving him, I felt huge pain for him. I saw his pain and it hurt me deeply. Out of all the men I had ever expressed the words "no" to, I had felt safe with him to express it from my truest authentic self.

"Please, no, not again, I can't bear it!" Totally disconnected from him and begging God from the surrendered part of me, as connecting to God was all I cared about. The part connected to God. Jack listened to me. He suddenly stopped and felt ashamed.

If I had always said no from this place, would the men in the past have listened?

After Jack had felt the full blunt force of my anger and hatred towards badly behaved men that had no respect for women; used them for sex and thought that was all they were good for; after his initial puppy dog sad look he stood up and made a phone call to one of his friends.

"It's an emergency, you have got to come here right now! You don't understand, I need you here right now!"

I was very confused and not really with reality and what was going on around me. I was simply happy and relieved to finally be near Rose's Jack again. I really believed he was my twin flame and eventually if I stayed with him long enough, he would see how amazing I was and how deep my love was for him. Everyone wants to be loved, don't they?

Eventually, his friend Ted, turned up. I had never met him before, I smiled and said "hello" I was being friendly and polite. Completely separated from the emotions I felt towards Jack.

Ted hadn't upset me; I had never met him before. I also knew I was in a situation where I needed to get at least one of his friends to like me, because friends are an important part of any person's life. I didn't want them all to hate me and eventually be kicked out forever! I had to love his friends too and show him I was a good person to be accepted and be in Jack's life too.

Ted nodded his head at me in response and said, "alright!"

I was incredibly happy to have someone new in the room to change the awkward atmosphere.

He looked at Jack to say, "What do you want? What is the matter?"

"You have got to help me; this girl is crazy! She just went completely crazy on me! I have a stalker!"

I completely surrendered and felt totally innocent. I was not going to let my ego react in any way. I wanted to be completely open, honest, and vulnerable. I knew I was in a desperate situation, but I didn't realise the extent until a bit later.

I am an actress; I made a look of "I don't know what he is talking about". I needed Ted on my side.

Anyway, I was innocent. I wasn't crazy. My behaviour looked crazy, I was releasing a lot of built-up angry resentment and unfortunately, he was the man that got the brunt of it because of his lies and manipulation. But it needed to be released.

Sex: Good or Bad?

"How does she know where you live?" Ted asked.

Jack looked guilty. Ted reacted with his body language and facial expression, "I see!"

"I didn't even have sex with her!" Jack stuck up for himself.

I made myself look innocent and shook my head to agree, feeling immensely proud of myself and letting it show.

I knew all my feelings were completely valid. Rori taught me and she taught me how to express them and I was doing so without any fear. I had no choice.

It was either to release all my feelings in a controlled manner and with awareness, or it was to continue bottling up my feelings and getting nowhere; going around in circles.

All though, this time I don't think I could have gone on in life any longer. I was really going crazy on the inside, internally. I had to feel the depth of my feelings, and I had to do it completely raw!

My interaction with Ted was different to my interaction with Jack. They were both separate from each other, and I wanted to create a unique experience with Ted.

After my sweet innocent look, Ted looked at Jack like he was confused and didn't understand either.

When Jack saw my reaction, he looked completely horrified. "No, wait! She is crazy! She just completely flipped out on me! She is an actress, and she is acting right now!" He then gave an impressed look, "she is a very good actress!"

I beamed with joy at his compliment on my acting skills. I surrendered to the love and joy I felt and let it wash through me. I was very much staying in the present moment and doing everything I could not to have any negative emotions. There was no need. I was in the presence of my one and only true love. My twin flame.

I was happy. My happiness depended solely on the presence of Rose's Jack. I felt I was nothing without him.

Jack looked frustrated and flustered and then remembered his other friend was there too. "I have a witness!" He said in a childish manner, like he was going to win this.

I had already won; he was standing in-front of me. He called his friend to join him in the doorway. They all stood staring at me sitting sweetly on the bed.

"She just went completely crazy at me, didn't she?"

I glanced a sweet innocent look at his friend, blushed and giggled in the most feminine flirty manner, in hope that he might not grass me up to the new friend, Ted.

He suddenly laughed and looked to the ground nodding his head at the nervous feelings inside him that I had made him feel. "Yes, yes she did!"

I then gave him a sarcastic smile to say, "thank you very much but not really!" Then I turned my head away in an immature childish grump.

"These are MY friends!" Jack said in disbelief that I was trying to steal his friendship group.

I couldn't believe it either and I knew it wouldn't happen. I just didn't know how else to be. I guess I was in a kind of strange survivors' mode. If I was a success in stealing his friends, then he would have to be my friend too. Or that was a weird belief I had at that time.

Ted went into the other room and again it was just three of us in Jack's room. Jack managed to say things to get an angry reaction out of me and I screamed at him again in pure anger and hatred.

"Teddy! Teddy! Did you see that? She went crazy again." He needed evidence to show Ted I was crazy.

Sex: Good or Bad?

Ted made an appearance and said, "Yes, yes I did, I heard that!" As if I was now in his bad books.

I felt disappointed and ashamed that I had let my anger get out of hand again and I surrendered, felt it fully and felt sad that he had heard me react so badly.

Ted then said to Jack, "This is just between you and her though, right?"

"I want you to help me get rid of her!" Jack said angrily!

Ted sort of stood in a soldier-like pose to say "yes sir" with a look of dread on his face.

I thought in an annoyed manner, "If he wanted me to just leave his apartment why didn't he just say?"

I can't remember how the conversation went after that exactly, but Jack was seated on the sofa again with his friend and Ted was in the other room.

At some point, I was shouting again and at another point, I was crying. I was feeling anything and everything and reacting with my truth to whatever Jack said.

I suddenly heard Jack roar in an angry rage, "I just want her to disappear forever!!"

I heard the message clearly that he really didn't want anything to do with me ever again.

I let the pain pierce through my heart and felt it in full force. My body drooped with it, sadness, pure heart-felt pathetic sadness. I started crying from the deepest saddest part of me. Disconnected from him and connected to only my emotion. Feeling safe alone with God.

"Ok," I said. From the same place when I had told him "No".

Pure sadness and realisation that I was going to be completely alone again. Complete unattachment. Freedom for him. The reality of how I felt about myself. Pathetic. So pathetic but I didn't care that anyone saw the truth of how I felt. Raw authentic patheticness. He looked at me and seemed to have feelings for me again. Sadness and pity. It was at least some sort of emotion from him. I didn't care if he was going to come for me or not. I have often wondered if he was just copying me to store it for later use on another victim. That is a possibility that has gone through my mind.

"Ok" I said again, "but please can I ask you for one thing? Please can I just stay here tonight?"

It was late and I guessed I had missed the last train home. If I hadn't, I felt so emotionally drained I could hardly function. I didn't have anywhere else to stay in the middle of London, apart from the streets. Not only was that going to be uncomfortable and cold, but I knew it would be dangerous. I could get raped or even murdered. I felt safe in the flat with Jack. Even if he didn't want me there.

"Ok," Jack agreed in an almost caring manner.

"Thank you," I wept in the gentlest manner.

I picked up my rucksack that I had my overnight stuff in to stay with Sara and went into the room where Ted was. Jack and his friend followed me in as I sat on the sofa.

I would stay the night like he said I could; on the sofa and leave as soon as I woke up in the morning. No dramas.

All three men were standing across the room from me. Jack had his arms crossed in-front of him in a stern manner. Jack said something that made me react again.

I wanted to launch myself at him this time and punch him; my whole body flinched to attack mode, but I refused to go totally unconscious. I wanted love. I wanted to be good in the eyes of God.

Sex: Good or Bad?

I threw my hands underneath me and firmly sat on them to keep them in place, while my legs were frantically thrashing in-front of me.

"Arrrrgh!" I roared. The anger was intense. I allowed it to express itself through me.

I finally managed to calm down again and get myself in a good place. I changed the present moment to love as my sweetheart was standing in front of me and he was allowing me to sleep the night.

Jack started saying how upset he was about what I did again.

"What did she do?" Ted asked. "She went around telling everyone that my name's not Rose's Jack!"

Ted looked interested! "How did she know that?"

"I don't know, maybe she's from the British government!"

This sounded like I could be exceptionally important. I matched the energy to the character and made myself look important as if I was from the government.

Jack scoffed, "she's not from the British Government!"

Worriedly Ted asked, "So what are you going to do now?"

"I don't know, I should kill her for what she did!"

My sarcastic ego that wanted to think he was really stupid, and that I was better than him reacted, "Go on then!" My body language said, "as if you're going to get away with that!"

He looked at me irritated like "What the fuck?"

Then he suddenly responded with his body language, "Ok, then I will!"

I suddenly remembered where I was and the Facebook status I had written before going around there.

Feeling the truth, was the only response I could think that might save me... I did it with a slight comedic tone to it. "Oh shit! What did you do that for, you stupid idiot?! Now what are you going to do? Oh great, I guess I you're about to die!!"

I couldn't think of anything else to do as I suddenly felt the feeling of pure horror fill my body. I was about to die. I was about to be murdered, helplessly in-front of bystanders.

I turned inward even deeper than I had before and even more pathetically in an act of total surrender in-front of Jack.

I blacked out from everyone and turned to God. "Ok, if this is my time, then so be it. I guess I am ready to meet you now."

I thought about my dad far away in Great Yarmouth with secondary cancer. He was nearing 80 and was probably at the end of his life. He promised me for years he would move to live nearer to me since my mother moved me away from him as a kid. I didn't feel like he really cared about me like I still yearned for him deep down. If he was going to die soon anyway, what was the point in me being alive?

Then I thought about my son, and I felt the deepest pain, and the deepest sadness. I felt so sorry for him without his mother.

I asked God to make sure he was happy and well looked after.

The pain of the thought of him not having me around was too much to bear, I was all he had.

I chose to believe that he would be OK, and everyone makes it to be ok, even me with all the pain I had endured in life. I was ok.

Even then, surrendered at the hands of a murderer. I was OK. I had God. I was surrendered to God.

Sex: Good or Bad?

CHAPTER 25

Twin Flame Hell Part 4

In the far distance, I heard a strong but muffled "no!"

The next part, I remember seeing Ted had a hold of Jacks' arm, my ego wants to describe it as pathetic,

"Please don't, she has a son; and she is really drunk, she doesn't know what she is doing!" Ted was begging him for my life.

The part of me that knows fear and courage, describes it as heroic and brave. The part of me that knows love and joy and wants to feel and express life, loves him, and cherishes him even to this day! Mostly I see this part of my life through ego eyes. Jack as the monster and Ted only wanting to have sex with me.

Jack was suddenly pulled out of his focus of what he was about to do to me, and he looked confused at Ted begging him not to. Confused that Ted was showing he had morals.

"What? "Do you like her?"

Ted put his head down in shame and nodded.

"What!? You like her?!"

Ted shamefully nodded again.

"You like her after what she did!"

Ted nodded and looked sorry for himself.

Sex: Good or Bad?

"Well, you have her then. Because I don't want her!" Jack said the second part of the sentence directed at me in anger and resentment.

I felt a deep sadness at those words. My heart was destroyed, and I couldn't process the part that happened before. I just stayed in the present moment, determined to feel love for my twin flame.

I couldn't believe he was going to pass me around to his friend like some sort of toy. My heart was devoted to Jack. I was still adamant that we were meant to be together. I felt so sad again.

"Wait until I tell Bethany Rose about this!" Jack spat in disgust.

"Why couldn't he just forget it now!" I thought. I suddenly flipped out again. I started shouting pure jealousy overrode me. I hated this girl. I hated that her name had the same word as Jacks'.

"Who cares about Bethany Rose! There is a fan in my bathroom called "man rose, Jesus was a man and he rose from the dead!" I was incredibly angry.

Ted, intrigued, asked Jack, "Why does she keep going on about the name Rose?"

Jack said in a worried and regrettable panic, "I called her an English Rose!"

Ted looked at me like I was remarkably interesting and mysterious. He couldn't wait to get to know me. Jack decided to suddenly call up Bethany Rose. He told the story of what I had done. Stalked him. Turned up unannounced. I stayed seated and calm.

"Whatever! I just wanted to sleep!" These were the thoughts that raced through my mind.

Jack then gave the phone to me, and Bethany Rose started shouting at me. My already damaged ego wanted to pretend that no one would ever find out about my visit, screamed at her. I pulled the phone away from my ear screaming at it, I was so angry I wanted to launch it across the room. I knew that was a violent thing to do and I didn't want to be violent. I looked at it, just screaming, not knowing what to do with my anger.

Jack suddenly came to me and said calmly and eagerly, "give me the phone, give me the phone!" Jack was close to me, and I instantly felt calm, and I wanted to please him. I gave him the phone and the external going on around me that made me react angrily, dissipated. I was desperate to be a good girl, especially in the eyes of God. I believed that Jack helped calm me.

Eventually it was just the four of us again. No one was on the end of any phone. I focussed on staying calm. The men spoke between themselves.

Jack then said, "Come on, let's go and get some food?" My past insecurities came up from past experiences. I imagined that they were planning to throw me out and they didn't want me there. I imagined that while we were out, they would run off and leave me to be all alone.

I snapped at them all, "Fine! I will go!" I picked up my rucksack and shouted again. "Take me to the train station NOW!"

Jack and Ted each took a step back looking horrified for a few seconds. The friend was shocked and wide-eyed too. There was a pause before Jack said, "No, I said we're going to go get food." I liked what he said but I didn't believe him, so I took my rucksack with me anyway because I didn't want to get locked out of the flat without it. We went to the pizza place and on the way passed Waitrose. Suddenly I saw a sign in this.

"Wait... Rose!" "Wait... Rose!" I was called an English Rose and I was supposed to wait until having sex! I suddenly started singing and dancing in the street with joy. I loved getting signs from God.

Sex: Good or Bad?

"You're not meant to do that in public," Jack said.

"But it is more fun in public" I said, not caring about what a fool I was going to make of myself in front of him. He had seen my worst side and he was allowing me to stay over again and be near him. I was excited! We then popped into the all-night corner shop run by a Muslim man.

Jack picked out a cushion with the Union Jack on it, all though it seemed to have a blood sort of stain look on it as part of the design. We went to the check out and Jack picked out a chocolate bar. He asked me if I wanted one. I smiled coyly at the thought of him buying me a gift. I melted with love.

The Muslim shop keeper asked Jack what was wrong with me. "Is she ok?"

I still wasn't with it. Still dissociated from the people around me. In an emotionally tired whirl wind, which had come to rest. The past few months had been agony and now I was with the man I had waited so long to be with again, releasing a lot of emotions to show him how I felt.

Jack said to the shopkeeper in annoyance, "Yeah! She went around telling people my name's not Roses' Jack.

The shop keeper then gave me an evil glare. I was oblivious to it though. I was with the man that I had yearned to be with for so long. I was tired and I was ready to sleep. When we walked back through the door of Jack's apartment, I caught a glimpse of myself in the hallway mirror. I had black mascara smudged all over my eyes from where I had been crying. I looked a mess.

I was mortified. I quickly put spit on my finger to try and rub it off before he came through the door. He smirked as I tried to pull myself together a bit. He had already seen what a mess I looked.

We sat on the bed, and they munched on pizza. I did not feel comfortable eating it. I had already intruded by wanting to stay the night. It had been a long time since I had used the toilet and I had drunk quite a bit of wine before showing up on his doorstep. I started making wobbly movements.

"What's the matter?" Jack asked, looking concerned.

"I really need a wee!" I yelled in frustration.

"Go! Go!" He quickly urged me to go to the toilet. I felt relieved when I got back, and I noticed there was one slice of pizza left. I looked excited and my reaction made it obvious that I wanted it but then I suddenly felt embarrassed and held back.

"Yes, you can have it!" Jack insisted.

I was enthusiastically happy. I sat on the bed, and I took a bite of pizza. Even though I was very hungry, I was too tired to wolf it down like I usually would have done. I chewed it slowly, emotionally drained in a slump but also tired. The alcohol high was wearing off and I was just sleepy.

Before taking another bite of the pizza I laid back and rested my head on the pillow. I was completely zoned out and I stared at the ceiling. I felt like a zombie. Just staring at the ceiling. I was tired and I wanted to move because I knew I must have made myself look even weirder but at the same time I was relaxed. I couldn't stop staring at the ceiling in a trance.

I suddenly had a flashback of when I felt this before. The film director. Sue the reiki healer had warned me about the film director. I suddenly remembered eating the pizza. I suddenly felt afraid that the pizza had been spiked. I didn't want to make it obvious what I thought though, in case I looked crazy for thinking that. I eventually pulled myself out of the zone and I sat up. Jack asked me if I wanted to finish the pizza. I made a face to say I couldn't be bothered which was partly true.

Sex: Good or Bad?

"No, thank you" I continued to be polite about it. Jack then pulled out what looked like a bottle of water, he said, "Do you want some of this? It is a drink!"

Again, I politely declined making the face to say I'd had enough. I then knew that he had spiked my pizza.

It was a horrifying feeling internally, but I pretended to myself that it was just a drink. He wasn't going to spike me, because that would be crazy! I eventually found myself next door ready to sleep on the sofa.

Teddy asked me if I wanted tea and for a split second, I was happy because I love tea and I always like to have fluid after drinking alcohol before sleeping. Then I remembered Jack trying to spike me, so I quickly retracted the excited feeling and suddenly scrunched up my face and said "no, thank you."

Ted asked me for my mobile number, and I gave it to him.

I went to sleep and woke up the next morning. Ted left and I waited to see if he was going to come back in. I wanted to be with Jack and only Jack. When it had been a few minutes I hovered outside his bedroom door, keen to be close to him again. We made eye contact, and he said I could go in which I did. I sat on the sofa, he was sat up in his bed and his friend was asleep next to him.

We had another interesting conversation with my interesting authentic reactions. He also said he had filmed me the evening before, and he was going to edit it and show everyone how awful I was. I didn't care. I was obviously an incredibly important human being if he was going to do that. I didn't know the people he was going to show it to, I wouldn't make it let me care.

All I cared about was him and being with him. Even though he showed me and clearly told me he wasn't interested in me. I eventually left, glad to have a reason to get away because I knew being needy and clingy was not attractive and I don't think I could have pulled myself away because I really didn't want to leave.

I wanted to stay with him forever and feel safe with him.

Crazy! He almost killed me!

After I left, I no longer cared about refraining from messaging him and I messaged him loads and loads. I didn't care if I was chasing him, I had to go with the flow and follow my feelings and what I wanted. I always tried to be funny in my messages and entertaining. I was never ever declaring my love or sending him hate messages and he never told me to stop sending them.

On occasions, I opened my heart out to a deep-feeling message. The way Rori taught me to feel and express my feelings. I was in pain, and I desperately wanted to be with him. I wanted to love him. I didn't care if he didn't love me back, all though his Instagram, which I fell hard for him over, showed he wanted love and his twin flame. I was adamant we were twin flames. Even though I knew the truth, my mind couldn't shake him off, all the feelings and pain were there like it was real. I never even had sex with him. After a few months, he eventually invited me over. I was ecstatic and over the moon. I was so happy! The wait was agonising. Ted was there too. He had moved and was living there. The story was his girlfriend had kicked him out.

To cut a long story short, I was there because Ted wanted me there. Jack and Ted both knew how I felt about Jack, and I knew how Ted felt about me. It was an extremely awkward situation but the way I felt for Jack was stronger than anything and I just wanted to be close to him; so, I always went along with it. Ted was always really kind and nurturing towards me and he made me feel comforted and loved. Feeding me and caring for me in different ways.I had forgotten about the near spiking incident. I wanted to play along like happy families, so desperately. As far as I am aware, I never got spiked by them. (Although, thinking about it, I did sleep very well on the sofa on the few times I did sleep over. I assumed it was because I was finally with my twin flame.)

Ted was gently soothing my pain. I was adamant I wouldn't fall for him, and because he was a man, I used all my feeling tools. It was natural for me to do at that point. It was easy, I didn't have to practise. They had both seen me in an awful state, yet I was still allowed to be in their company. Ted still liked me and wanted to see me; the crazy state I was in, I still had them as company. I was still quiet though because I still wasn't 100% comfortable. I wasn't sure if they actually did want me there. Of course, Jack did trivial things to try and hurt me, I don't blame him. Some men only know how to relate to a woman by hurting them, but I didn't feel pain, I only felt love. I was with my twin flame. All I felt was love, I felt like I was at home. I felt relieved every time I got to be with him.

The only pain I felt was when we were separated, and I didn't know when or if I would get to see him again and he wouldn't reply to any of my messages. Ted came and met me a couple of times and took me out for dinner.

Once I got to be with Jack alone in his flat and we had a conversation. (In desperation I sent him an explicit poem about sucking his dick.)

He was shocked to hear that Ted had met me twice in my hometown and had even taken me out to dinner.

"He took you out for dinner!" He said, looking very shocked! I nodded like it was no big deal. "You've got him wrapped around your little finger, haven't you?"

I smiled a little uncomfortable, but I also felt pleased. I shrugged my shoulders because I didn't know if I did have him wrapped around my little finger.

"Yes, you have. What are you going to do with him now?" I wasn't sure, I shrugged my shoulders and made an uncomfortable grimace face. He asked me if anything happened between us. I told him we kissed.

"You kissed him! Oh my god! I can't believe you kissed him!" He sounded like I had cheated on him or something.

"Yeah!" I refused to feel confused about this. I knew he knew he wasn't in a relationship with me, and I knew he knew that Ted liked me.

"You kissed him! Do you like him?" The word "like" always confuses me because it is pretty bland, but people use it for potential romantic relationships. You wouldn't have non-romantic friends you don't like and, it's not nice to not like people you're interacting with... so, it is pretty confusing. If you don't like someone, you wouldn't interact with them.

I said, "Yeah, I like him. He is my friend. Just like you're my friend!" Reminding him that he is just my friend too, so him being jealous would be weird. He had made it clear he didn't want me. Even though at any given chance I couldn't help but take myself to be near him.

I remember starting to feel more confident around Jack and I started being able to have moments of really feeling. The feeling of love flowed through me. I felt relaxed because he was near me.

I remember he said, "it's not going to work on me!" Then I felt the deep sad part authentically. I could see him react and a twitch melting through his eyes.

One of the times I was alone with him. We were sitting on separate sofas, and I was feeling such a wave of lightness, love, and comfort.

"Stop that!" He suddenly said.

I wasn't aware I was doing anything. I was enjoying the moment in his company feeling pure love but not attaching it to him. I was feeling and flowing, inner beauty essence. "Stop what?" I was confused. I wasn't aware I was doing anything.

"That, stop that! You know what!"

"I don't know," I said innocently.

"That! Stop what you're doing right now!"

I suddenly felt grumpy because I didn't know what he was talking about. I crossed my arms and leaned over in a strop, with my face matching my feelings.

Jack suddenly looked away and bit his lip, with a small smile on his face.

After a few moments of silence he said, "Ok, you can do it!"

"Do what?"

"Whatever you want to do you can just do it!" I was so pleased with his words, I stretched myself out on the sofa, feeling relieved, the love and energy flowing through me again. This time it felt a little more intense due to the contrast I was feeling before. Jack took a breath himself and looked intrigued. Looking back, I am guessing I made him feel something. Looking back, I wonder if that made me dangerous to him.

He certainly got a kick out of my negative reactions when they occurred. I kind of did too in a strange sort of way. I was able to release negative reactions I felt from the past. I never ever blamed him, and I always found a higher reason as to why I would be reacting in so much pain, by welcoming it and surrendering to it, to let it go.

It took about 2 years until I was finally able to stop contacting him and the constant thinking died down. At Christmas I sent him a parcel full of well-thought-out presents, lots of little gifts I thought he might like or find useful. I just wanted to love, and instead of trying to hold myself back I did so without expecting anything in return. He thanked me for the Christmas presents.

The hope was there that I would hear from him after I sent more gifts to him on Valentine's day but he helped by not responding to me.

Each day and each month got easier and easier until I felt OK to bury whatever it was that held me onto him. I managed to bury the rest of the left-over pain needed to process and get on with my life.

My father came to live with me for three months before he passed away from cancer and it was the best distraction ever. I loved and adored him with all my heart and did everything I possibly could to keep him comfortable.

Not long after my father passed away, I found an article on Facebook I was drawn to read. It led me onto buying a book called "Complex PTSD; from Surviving to Thriving." Author Pete Walker. (I highly recommend this book for people that have SURVIVED trauma. Survivor is present tense, the trauma that happened was in the past. Thank you, Adam Mussa.) After clicking on the website and ordering the book I had many adverts pop up on my news feed to do with PTSD and healing.

I ended up going to a free event where a speaker was going into detail about all his experiences. At the end of this event, he wanted to speak to me. He asked me to follow him on Instagram. I noticed that a very well-known person that had followed me was following him too.

This "celebrity" was also a friend of Jacks.' I was automatically in awe. A weird energy started to lift around me. I felt like I was safe with him as he had also been through many traumatic experiences. The rest of the pain that I had buried that hadn't been able to be released with the experience I had with Jack, came to the surface. I believed that Jack was my false twin flame and perhaps this new guy was my real twin flame.

Sex: Good or Bad?

Funny, I thought the film director had been my false twin flame when I met Roses' Jack.

The painful experience with Jack was repeated. It was still intense, but it was nothing like the experience with Jack. Eventually, any trapped pain I experienced from the past disappeared completely.

I met a wonderful man called Philip Chan a few weeks after meeting the speaker. He was an incredibly good friend to me, and we spoke every night on the phone during the first few months of the coronavirus lockdown. He made me feel loved. I felt he was the only person I had that really cared about me, and he was there and did what he could to make me feel safe.

However, as a person with a traumatic past I wasn't 100% able to feel it with a man that was truly safe. When shown love I was used to showing hate; when shown hate I was used to showing love.

One day I called Philip up, crying hysterically on the phone to him, "Who loves you?" He asked me.

"Philip loves me," I replied. He used to tell me every night on the phone that my son Alfie loves me, Philip loves me, and I have lots of family and friends that love me and my dad's love will always be there. He was the sweetest, gentlest and kindest man. All I knew was that Philip was always there if I called him and he had a lot of time for me. He really was one of a kind and a wonderful man.

I met up quite a lot with my now husband during this time. The power of feeling loved and being able to trust it and let it in was a true miracle for me.

Thank you, Philip Chan, you will forever be adored and loved by everyone that knew you.

I was heartbroken to hear that he died one week before my

wedding from Coronavirus or from the underlying conditions he had. I wondered if I had a part in it, I knew he loved me. I am sorry Philip if I broke your heart. Philip taught me the Honopono poem. "I'm sorry, Frankie. Please forgive me Frankie, I love you Frankie, Thank you Frankie." I am sharing it with anyone in a state of heartache and desperation. Say these words and you too will grow to feel better.

Philip passed away in October 2021. I heard he was in his 70's and had been unwell for a very long time. I remember him taking part in a 25 push-ups everyday challenge on Facebook during the first lockdown in 2020. That is how powerful Philip was.

I know you're experiencing the place indescribable with words, you were always the most amazing and beautiful-hearted man. Philip's love with always be there.

Many times in my life I have realised that I have said, "I'm sorry God, please forgive me God, thank you God, I love you God".

I met Philip in December 2019. I had reverted to Islam in July 2019. Philip said that he had an amazing feeling when he met me. He said only one other time in his whole life had he had that feeling. It was when he was in a room full of nuns. When I first entered the room full of people, I had my head covered. I took the head scarf off through, feeling nervous being the only one in the room with it on.

Philip was an amazing hearted man. He believed the feeling he experienced was because of Nuns and because of me. I believe the feeling was him, already in him. I felt afraid when he said those words to me as it was a very good feeling, and I still felt very cautious of him because of past manipulations. However, now he is gone I realise how special he really was.

Sex: Good or Bad?

CHAPTER 26

Another Heavenly experience

I had this experience while I was desperately trying to stop being head crazy over Roses' Jack. The guy that I had opened my heart up to fully, and felt the deepest love for (which I had attached to him, but I now realise that love is me, in me, always.)

I had attached the love to him, and I felt immense pain, which I now see was needed in order for me to process all the past trapped pain. Pain that I had never felt safe to feel before because I'd had sex with them.

It had been some time. I knew Jack had lied to me to get my barriers down wasn't going to come around and give me the marriage he promised me.

I started dating again and meeting other men. I was desperate to try and get the evil man out of my head and to stop the pain with a distraction.

I found myself in bed with a really lovely kind caring and sweet gentle man.

A man that knew how to love, but the childhood, adolescent and adult traumata I experienced meant I wasn't able to accept it, and it felt unsafe, like he had an alternative agenda for being kind to me (which is exactly the guys I used to fall for anyway). When it was genuine it was far too scary.

I had gotten myself drunk because I had felt afraid, and I felt like I had to let him perform a sexual act on me and have sex with him. This was not true. The fear was because of my experiences with past men not accepting my "no".

While he was performing the sexual act, I had my eyes closed like I sometimes would do, and I was enjoying the physical sensations.

I suddenly remembered Jack who I allowed to fully crack open my heart to love at the deepest part of me, I remembered him, and my heart suddenly cracked open. I felt the most beautiful awe-inspiringly love feeling take over my whole body. It was so beautiful that tears fell from my eyes and rolled down my cheeks. It wasn't anything like the light experience, after I met with the reiki healer, Sue, but it was still a deeply beautiful and magical experience.

I believed it was because I had thought of the guy that cracked me open to love, I believed it should have been him there with me; I believed the love I was feeling came from my heart and was directed to him; but after contemplating on this, and I even asked the gentleman sometime after, I reminded him of this moment.

I asked him. "Were you loving me?"

He assured me that he had been genuine. I realise now, my heart had cracked open, and I was in a safe place, I was in such a safe place and the love was real, that the emotion overwhelmed me and made me cry.

My heart had been cracked open and I was receiving love from him. The love that was inside my heart, I should have been able to give that love to the man that was loving me in that moment, but I was unable to.

I was open to the love from his heart coming my way and it brings a tear to my eye now remembering it.

I didn't feel able to communicate to him what I was feeling. He asked me if I was OK to which I replied with a nod of the head.

Afterwards he sent me downstairs to the spare room, which he may have done to be kind and caring to me, but I thought he was rejecting me. I yearned for him to hold me in his arms. I guess he put me in the spare room because he wasn't expecting sex from me at all.

That is a kind gentleman thing to do that can make a woman feel extra safe and comfortable.

I should have felt safe enough not to drink alcohol and safe enough to make it clear I will not have sex with him. I should have felt good enough in myself to know he must have been feeling wonderful just having me there.

Yes, I was very drunk and perhaps he shouldn't have had sex with me, but I think he knew why I was drinking the alcohol and he was just following his manly instincts. I had made up my mind to have sex with him to make him happy. For some reason a part of me felt guilty if I didn't. I don't regret it and if I had been in a better place emotionally and mentally, he could have been the man I ended up marrying. He wasn't of course, it wasn't meant to be.

CHAPTER 27

Step by Step Summary

1. Connect to your deepest inner self. (Or God.) Surrender. Admit where you made mistakes in the past. Affirm to change it.

2. Dress up to feel good for your own self and take yourself out on dates.

3. Be aware of any thoughts or beliefs you have about the opposite sex and realise they're from your past experiences, and know that by generalising about a whole group is always going to be false

4. Practice on all members of the opposite sex that you meet. Rejection isn't scary when you own yourself and feel connected and know there are many others to interact with. Welcome any rejections and feel the truth if it hurts.

5. Give members of the opposite sex a chance, where you wouldn't normally.

6. Trust yourself and your boundaries.

7. When you start to get to know a member of the opposite sex. Communicate what it is exactly that you're after. (Not on the first date, I did this once and never heard from the guy again. I assumed he wanted sex right away, so I needed to protect myself. I should have gone with the flow of my feelings, been honest and fearless, and enjoyed each

moment.)

8. Never be afraid of scaring the opposite sex away. (You can even use this in the practice phase. Aim to scare them away and see what happens!)

9. Anything you don't like, remember, "What we see in others is a reflection of ourselves." That is exactly the same for when you like someone a lot. Remember you're a perfect being, living a human experience and we evolve by interacting with others, however difficult it may seem at times.

10. Remember that the opposite sex needs to feel safe. Men feel it by a woman being able to really feel into her real feelings. A woman can feel that way by being genuinely cared for by a man with no pressure of sex!

11. Remember your spouse doesn't want to hurt you on purpose, so be cautious and careful about your negative responses to any situation. Negative reactions can trigger an even more negative situation. If they do seem to hurt you on purpose and you feel trapped, pray to God for a righteous way out.

12. Always aim to come from a place of love. Love for yourself and love for the other. Aim to give love rather than take love. If you give too much without giving to yourself, take yourself away to give yourself love and attention. If things ever feel rocky, go back to steps 1 and 2 of this summary chapter. Re-read the chapters "Toxic", and "Ego".

13. Remember... If you ever feel unloved... I LOVE YOU!

CHAPTER 28

Stella Talk Show Host Q&A

1. Why do you say that some women that reveal skin feel insecure?

When a woman becomes brave and feels able to reveal a lot of skin, it is powerful, but then thought can come into it... If there is a thought they have about doing it, it can then become a reason for why they are doing it, and then it loses its power.

Especially if the thought is, "I will capture a man's attention" or "I feel good, so I look good". The ego becomes aware of the power, "I am powerful for doing this!"

When the thought process comes in of how we look, it is then an ego identity.

The thought process comes in of how they look, and it takes them away from feeling into their essence.

If their thought process is "I will capture a man's attention" or "I will be more attractive to a man", then they are not secure enough in their personality or their powerful feminine essence, they believe they need to look their very best, and by doing so reveal skin.

Also, I speak about being soft and vulnerable in my book, and unfortunately in my experience, and what I have personally seen in the world at this point in time, it is still not completely safe.

I remember a comment from a male to another male, "I couldn't understand why suddenly there were so many attractive women around that I hadn't noticed before. Then I realised it was spring and summer and, in the winter, they are all covered up."

Even a strong woman with strong boundaries, that attracts a man, there is a risk she may subconsciously feel guilty for attracting him and may have a false inkling that he is entitled to her.

Until the dangerous toxic ego in too many men has been dissipated (if possible with evolution and awakening), women are not 100% safe.

I remember a conversation I had with a male friend, that has never felt successful with the ladies, he was all for ladies showing some skin. I couldn't help but wonder if he enjoyed looking at them as it was his only way to get some sexual enjoyment.

If porn and glamour models didn't exist and women did fully cover, men would have no choice but to put a lot of effort in to win a woman over, hunt her down to get what he needs, which is sex or in nicer words, love and connection.

I do have another view that if everyone walked around naked, all of the time, then nakedness would be normal, but because of porn and strippers etc, a naked person, especially a female is automatically seen as something sexual.

Then again, it could just be nature, even a breast feeding woman is told to cover up, sex creates babies, a woman breast feeding her baby may subconsciously be seen as sexual, or again, maybe it is just because of porn and glamour models?

If a breast feeding mother is seen as something sexual because of nature, then that is actually truly beautiful, because any mother knows how incredible it is to be a mum. Pure love and connection, which is what sex is supposed to be for.

2. You have a son and did have while going through the twin flame hell, how were you able to handle being a mother whilst going what you went through?

Sex: Good or Bad?

My one-word answer is, God! Even though I felt extremely disconnected, I knew God was there somewhere.

My answer feeling extremely guilty about it all -

It was an extremely dark time and I barely felt like I was surviving. Because I hadn't chosen the best father figure role model for my son, I felt like a bad mother. I always longed for us to have a strong male in our lives, a hero, to rescue us, to feel loved and cared for.

I realise now, that because I was lucky enough to have such a wonderful father growing up, I thought that is how love is supposed to be. As a child, love to me was my father, my protector, I would run to him away from the bullies and away from anyone wanting to cause me harm. I felt the comfort and safety of his presence and thought that is how love should feel. After doing Abdul Mussa's course I discovered that even as adults' people that survived childhood abuse, we long for that feeling, but it isn't appropriate, because we are not children anymore.

Even though I knew everything I had learnt that desperation took over me, I was desperate to have a complete family, Mum, son and Dad.

Because of the trauma I endured at the hands of men, I couldn't trust any man and I felt alone and afraid. So, when I met the man I believed to be my "twin flame" I allowed myself to go fully dependent on him, believing I could trust him and be with him. Something else trauma survivors do is either blindly trust or blindly distrust, and neither is a good idea.

I am so relieved when I look back on that time that we made it through, because it felt like it was never ending.

The main thing is my son knows I love him and adore him. He knows he is loved. Just like I knew my dad loved me.

My son has ASD and neither of his schools helped us much. I really struggled knowing my son could do so much better, if he had the support he needed.

Another book I write will be "Autism at Mainstream school."

My husband has been amazing supporting me and he guided me, and because of him, having a wonderful man in my life, my son has now been awarded an Education, health and care plan. He can get into a specialist school with that, and he will have all the support he needs.

I believe deep down, women need men in their life. I know I always did, and I am blessed with the one I have. Men need women and women need men, and we must learn to listen to each other, and see and appreciate every little thing each other does.

I believe I had to go through the twin flame hell, so then I could finally make the decision to be with a man that will never hurt me. I love God and I am grateful for God's love and mercy, and I am so happy to have completed half my deen.

Printed in Great Britain
by Amazon